Where do you live? Peoria? Salt Lake City? Birmingham? Kankakee? Spokane? Buffalo? Memphis? No. No, you don't. You don't live in any of those places or in any other place that has a name. You live, night and day, week after week, year in and year out, in the nameless hidden places of your mind.

The creators of the CBS Radio Mystery Theater invite you to expand your consciousness and explore those hidden places in three of the strangest tales ever to be told by outstanding authors of the macabre. . . .

TIME AND AGAIN
THE BLACK ROOM
THE ONLY BLOOD

Strange
tales
from
CBS
Radio
my tery
theater

edited by Himan Brown

POPULAR LIBRARY · NEW YORK

STRANGE TALES
FROM THE
CBS RADIO
MYSTERY THEATER

E. G. MARSHALL:	THE CBS RADIO MYSTERY THEATER PRESENTS:
SOUND:	THE CREAKING DOOR (8 seconds)
MUSIC:	THEME (10 seconds) AND UNDER FOR
E. G. MARSHALL:	(ON CUE) Come in ... Welcome ... I am E. G. Marshall, Curator of the little Museum of the Macabre—with another adventure so strange and so chilling that we dare say you'll get little sleep this night.

"We're rolling," says Fred Himes, my engineer. Marlin Swing, the Assistant Director, starts his stop watch, nods to me and I throw the first cue to E.G. Marshall. On the word "presents", Pete Prescott, the sound effects man punches the cartridge button for the sound of the creaking door. There is eight seconds of agonizing and almost unbearable squeaks and groans from the oh-so-familiar door. I snap "Hit music" to the engineer, and the ominous notes of our theme segue with the final creaks of the door, and swell for ten seconds. As the music goes down, I again cue E.G. and we are off to another adventure in the macabre.

This is the pattern I have been following for almost three years, seven nights a week at six minutes after the on-the-hour news. On 225 stations "the spoken word" once again is heard by more than fifteen million listeners. People are once again listening to radio. If you stop to think of it you'll have to admit that "listening" has become a lost art these days. Who really listens? Because, really, who has to?

In the late fifties it was decided that you couldn't broadcast dreams on the air unless you transmitted pictures with it. This, despite the fact that radio had become the most popular mass entertainment medium of all time. The basic appeal of radio drama was the fact that you had to listen if you wanted to follow it. It wasn't enough to merely "hear" it. You had to listen. The word listen implies a conscious effort to pay attention, to participate. Thus, all the senses are activated, the curiosity is sparked, the imagination is fired, and the listener finds himself participating. In a real sense, he is a collaborator. In his brain he matches a face and a body to the voice. In his mind, he sees the action. And this is the basic difference between radio on the one hand, and every visual medium on the other. A good movie, a fine stage play or television drama, an excellent ballet, all these require an appreciative audience—but only radio calls for a creative audience—a listener who literally works with the writer, the director, the actors and technicians to give completeness to the creative process.

It can fairly be said that along about the same time that radio drama disappeared, there came about a general decay in the art of listening. If you don't believe it, "listen" to some of the nonsense that's being spouted in all fields of endeavor and in all walks of life. This kind of talk is being inflicted upon us because, in my opinion, people aren't really listening.

The most popular word in our language is now Communication. We deplore the fact that we no longer seem to be able to communicate with our children, our parents, our government, our allies, industry, labor, each other.

How can we communicate if we no longer listen? A radio show has listeners, a television show has "viewers". Listening is an activity. Viewing is an event. Of course, there is room and need for all the entertainment media—and happily, a regrettable error made some two decades ago is slowly and hopefully being rectified. To me, it was incomprehensible that a flourishing and, yes, a spiritually nourishing, art form should have been allowed to die. I had created, produced and directed such radio classics as INNER SANCTUM MYSTERIES, NERO WOLFE, THE THIN MAN, BULLDOG DRUMMOND, GRAND CENTRAL STATION, DICK TRACY, TERRY AND THE PIRATES, and an endless number of other serials and documentaries. I was determined to see radio drama once again an integral part of broadcasting. But it took fourteen years of constant and insistent knocking at the doors of networks, agencies and sponsors. It wasn't until I reached Sam Cook Digges, President of CBS Radio, who, it turned out, was as great a fan as I am, that things began to happen. He created the CBS DRAMA NETWORK and the first series for that network was born—THE CBS RADIO MYSTERY THEATER.

An entire new generation has "discovered" radio drama and fallen in love with this new "art" form. For earlier generations there is the equally exhilarating experience of "re-discovery". Hundreds of thousands of letters have been sent to us, all of them thanking us for giving the listeners an "alternative to television." Thanking us for once again making the "theater of the imagination" a part of their lives. Making us more aware than ever that the word is "listeners". And because radio drama develops this capacity to derive entertainment and enlightenment through listening, we shall all be the better for it.

At this time, more than five hundred original stories have been written on special assignment for the CBS RADIO MYSTERY THEATER. Many of them deserve a place in this anthology. But there is room for only three. There are those who will claim that there are at least a hundred others every bit as good, if not better, than the ones I have chosen. And they may be right. Therefore, it has been with considerable soul-searching that I finally selected the three you are about to read. In all cases, a selection process is highly subjective—and in the end, I admit, I liked these for a variety of personal reasons.

"THE ONLY BLOOD" is by Sam Dann, who goes back with me to the early days of radio. Although he is active in other media—the stage and television—radio was his first love. He has written many excellent stories for our series. I have chosen "THE ONLY BLOOD" for a number of reasons. First, it is an exciting and touching story. Second, it is at its core, a morality play. It deals with the basic responsibility of the individual. And just as O'Henry and DeMaupassant could sum up the meaning of an entire story in a final, revealing sentence, here in the very last line spoken by Anthony Boda, Sam Dann illuminates the basic difference between a man of good and a man of evil. Third, I have a personal feeling for the time and place. This is obviously a story of the thirties and it takes place in a melting pot. I myself knew people like these; lived among them. All of these scenes figured significantly

11

in my own growing up. This is when I entered radio and began to make my own way. I feel a part of this story—and I am sure you will, too.

It was the ill-fated Prince of Denmark, Hamlet, who lamented, "The time is out of joint! O cursed spite that I was ever born to set it right!"

Many people, before and since, and without doubt in the long future, have, and will, echo that same cry of despair. But none with more justice than Ethan Vigil, clockmaker by profession, and avenging angel of destruction by compulsion and accident. Ian Martin tells his story in "TIME AND AGAIN". He assured me that he could vouch for the story because the manuscript from which he wrote the story fell into his hands by luck or chance, however you like to treat the meaning of those words. Ian Martin cannot resist an auction. (Neither can I.) Which is how he happened to possess the curious document he first dramatized for me on the CBS RADIO MYSTERY THEATER. Here now you can read, in its original form, this bone-chilling account of how many lives were lost to the inhuman demands of what Ethan Vigil himself termed: "This damnable machine".

The manuscript speaks for itself, even if Ian Martin could not always manage to decipher the cramped longhand. The basic agony and the terrible cry for understanding and forgiveness will always echo in my heart, as hauntingly as this strange record will, down the halls of time. Ethan Vigil, as you will read, was a man caught in a terrifying circumstance—a circumstance I can hope you will only dream about—but never find in actuality. Because none of us can resist the fascination of time—our never-ending quest to find a special way to hoard it, stretch it, somehow arrest its inevitable march—and, in some way, to borrow a little extra portion of it for ourselves. Haven't you, as I have, had the irrational impulse to hold our hand against the clock's face and to bring it to a stop—to bring time itself to a stop?

Resist the impulse!

Wind your watches and your clocks. Let them run their course.

Once around is enough—or should be—for all of us.

Elspeth Eric, author of "THE BLACK ROOM", worked for me as an actress all through the forties and fifties. She always wanted to write and one day I was surprised by her announcement that she was one of the writers for an important daytime television soap. It was only a step to ask her to write for me as one of the "regulars" of the CBS RADIO MYSTERY THEATER.

Her story "THE BLACK ROOM" is a departure from the usual run of dramas I present. It is the story of one man's struggle against nervous collapse—a most difficult subject to dramatize. It is not a story of horror or of wonder. It is the story of a human being alive, but split off from life, sentient but not living. There is nothing superior or even remarkable about the man himself. He has no magic powers, no super-human resources—he is Anyman.

"THE BLACK ROOM" echoes the real-life experiments of a few years ago where men were totally submerged in water, provision made only for their bodily existence. It is interesting to note that at the end of a prolonged underwater period, pages from the telephone book were read to them. To a man, all declared that the reading was the most beautiful sound they had ever heard.

I am certain that you will enjoy reading these three engrossing and unusual stories. And I invite you (if you aren't already an avid fan) to join the millions who listen nightly for the creaking door to open with another CBS RADIO MYSTERY.

The Black Room

Elspeth Eric

Where do you live? Peoria? Salt Lake City? Birmingham? Kankakee? Spokane? Buffalo? Memphis? No. No, you don't. You don't live in any of those places or in any other place that has a name. You live, night and day, week after week, year in and year out, in the nameless hidden places of your own mind.

* * * * * * * * *

Two men are walking down a shaded street bordered by neat, attractive houses, similar but not identical, set on half-acre lots and all tidily landscaped. The short plump man looks steadily at the sidewalk; the other, a head taller, bends over a little as he asks earnestly, "Why this one, Mr. Zee?"

"Why not this one?" Zee still staring at the sidewalk as it disappears beneath their feet.

"What do you know about him?"

Zee shrugs. "Enough."

17

"How much is enough?" The tall man persists.

"Nothing would be plenty since they're all the same. But probably it's better to have one with some slight powers of reflection and evaluation. This one has."

"What does he do for a living?"

"Advertising, I believe. Something on that order."

"Educated?"

"College degree. B.A."

"Family?"

"Wife, anyway. Why are you pestering me, Kay?"

Unabashed the tall man says, "I like to know these things."

"They don't really matter. You should know that by now."

The tall man called Kay persevered. "How successful is he?"

"Knowing such things—even being interested in such things—only opens the door to personal interest and possible attachment. Yes, he's moderately successful."

"Intelligent then?"

"The one doesn't necessarily follow the other." The contempt in Mr. Zee's voice is just barely discernible.

"One more thing. Will he cooperate?"

"How in the world would I know that so early in

the game?" The short plump Mr. Zee gave a little snort. "Forgive me, Kay, but sometimes—"

"That's all right. They all cooperate."

"Up to a point."

"At the beginning they all do. I wonder why that is." Kay's look is contemplative.

"Because they trust us."

"Why do they?"

"Some vestige remains from childhood, I suspect."

"That must be it."

"Here's the house." The stodgy man turns abruptly up a flagstone walk and Kay, after a little lurch, follows. At the front door of the white clapboard house, he lifts and lets fall the shiny brass knocker. Then they both stand, hands in pockets, somber waiting.

"Oh, one more thing," says Kay.

"What now?"

"How old?"

"Thirty-four. The right age for questioning."

"Why is that?"

"It's the year when youth ends. Didn't you know?"

The door opens and a man looks out. He is dressed in gray slacks, a blue shirt and brown loafers. His russet hair is slightly rumpled and his blue eyes, inquisitive.

"We wondered could you help us out," says the short plump man.

19

"That depends," the man smiles a friendly smile.

"We're looking for information." Mr. Zee pulls a card encased in leather and cellophane from his pocket. Cupped in his hand, he holds it out. The man glances at it briefly. "If I can help—"

"We think you can."

"What's it about?" the man asks.

"Would you mind coming down to headquarters? We'll fill you in down there. Privately."

"Well sure. If you'll wait a sec—"

"You won't need a coat."

"My wife—"

"This won't take long. A few simple questions."

"Well if it won't take long—"

"You'll be back before you know it."

"Well, always glad to help."

"Thanks very much. Appreciate it."

The man closes the door behind him. He smiles an amiable smile at the other two. There is a measure of conspiracy in the smile like that of a young boy setting off with friends on a prank. The other two smile but gravely. A bit jauntily the three start off.

"No car?" the man asks.

"It isn't far," says Mr. Zee.

"I've never been asked to do anything like this before," the man says.

"We wouldn't trouble you if we didn't need the information. Really need it, I mean."

"Oh, I'm sure you wouldn't," the man says hastily. "I just hope I have it."

The three walk on for half a block or so in silence. Then the man says, "Who told you—what gave you the idea that I might? Have the information?"

"We still don't know for sure that you do." The boxy little man looks solemn.

"I don't get around much, you know. I lead a very—a very ordinary sort of life. Very circumspect. I don't have any criminal contacts. Not that I know of anyway." The man's little chuckle is meant to be ingratiating.

"That's not necessary."

"Well then. Why me?"

"Long shot. Off-chance."

"Kind of exciting," says the man.

The three walk on without speaking till the plump man says, "We're here. We've arrived." All three turn in at a brick building that might once have been a factory. They climb an old flight of stairs and enter a room with the look of an office, being painted the noncommittal shade of green that offices seem to call for. There is a flattopped desk with nothing on it and a chair behind it, a standing lamp of uncertain age and design and that is all. The short Mr. Zee seats himself behind the desk; the tall Mr. Kay stands in front of the only door other than the one by which they entered; their guest stands, awkwardly at first, then leans against the desk and slightly over it,

21

looking expectantly at Mr. Zee who says, "Sorry. We're short on furniture."

"You said this wouldn't take long." The man smiles easily.

"Not if we come straight to the point."

"Fine by me."

Mr. Zee leans forward across the desk. "Tell me. What are you afraid of?"

The man pulls back, straightens up. "How's that?"

From behind him comes the voice of Mr. Kay. "What are you afraid of?"

"Am I supposed to be afraid of something?" The man is still smiling. "I think you've got the wrong man."

"No we haven't," says Mr. Zee from behind the desk.

"I don't have anything to be afraid of."

"It doesn't follow that you're not afraid of anything."

"Look, I thought this was going to be some kind of criminal investigation."

"Not strictly."

"Then what is it?" The man's voice holds a note of irritability.

"An investigation of your private fears, you might say."

"What for?"

"Because we're interested."

"Interested in me? Why me specifically?"

"Not you *specifically*. Human fears in general."

"That's rot," says the man, "Stuff and nonsense." He has not lost completely his look of affability, he only looks puzzled and mildly perturbed. "Like everybody says, I have nothing to hide. At least that's what I imagine everybody says."

"Everybody does say that." Mr. Zee manages a wizened smile.

"Well, most people don't have anything to hide."

"All people do." Mr. Zee retains his tiny smile.

"Nothing that's against the law. Nothing you'd be interested in."

"We have nothing to do with the law."

"But you said—I thought you said—"

"Did we say we had anything to do with the law?"

"I just assumed—you flipped that card at me—I took it for granted that you—and the way you talked—"

"Did we ever at any time say we had anything to do with the law?"

"Maybe not in so many words—" The man's voice is showing anger.

"Did the card I showed you indicate that we had anything to do with the law?"

"I didn't actually *read* it, people don't *read* those things. I just thought of course you were from the FBI."

"Oh, no!"

"Well the CIA then. Something official. Something—you know—legitimate."

"We are not official." Mr. Zee leans further across the desk. "And not strictly legitimate. Or illegitimate either, for that matter."

"Then what the hell are you?"

"Let's get back to the questions." Mr. Zee settles back in his chair. "Once you've answered them we'll part company and you can go home."

"You ask damn silly questions."

"You give damn silly answers."

"There are no answers to the questions you ask."

"There must be."

"I don't know what must be. I only know—"

Mr. Kay takes a few steps toward the desk. "He'll never tell you."

The man's affability has given way to exasperation flecked with apprehension. "What am I supposed to be afraid of?"

"That's for you to tell us."

"Screw you!"

"He's hopeless," Mr. Kay says almost sadly.

"You guys—" The man's eyes travel from the one to the other. "Who the hell are you anyway?"

Zee speaks softly, gently. "I'm the man in charge here."

"What's he? The big one?"

"My deputy."

"What are you in charge of? Who gave you the

right to bust into my house and drag me down here?"

"We didn't bust in and we didn't drag you."

"Whatever."

"Actually, if we'd had time to wait, you might have found your way here all by yourself."

"Fat chance!"

"It's been known to happen."

"I never knew you even existed till a little while ago." Any trace of geniality has left the man by now and desperation is setting in. "Can I make a phone call?" he asks.

"I'm afraid not," Mr. Zee says quietly.

"Everybody's allowed to make a phone call."

"Out of the question. We have no phone."

"I never heard of a place that had no phone."

"Well, now you have."

The man is sweating. "You can't keep me here."

"Why not?"

"Because you can't. It's not right."

Mr. Zee's voice is still kind and gentle, even solicitous. "What's your idea of what's right? We'd really like to know."

"Don't be silly," the man says impatiently. "I can't give you a definition off-hand like that."

Then, even softer, gentler, kindlier. "You mean against regulations, don't you? Against the rules?"

"Something like that maybe."

25

"Is all life so regulated? So prescribed?" Zee asks earnestly.

"You're mixing me up."

"Too bad. I'd meant to clarify if I could." Now, briskly, "Mr. Kay, I think it's time for The Black Room."

The man says, "Wait a second, just wait one damned second—"

"Come with me please." Kay's tone is firm but deferential.

"Come with you where?"

Kay holds the door open, makes a polite little bow.

The man says, "I'm not going anywhere with you."

Kay grows slightly impatient. "Come on, come on," he says.

"I don't have to. You can't make me."

"Yes, you do. And yes, we can."

The man turns toward the desk. "Do I have to?"

Mr. Zee answers with something like compassion. "Yes, you do."

"Right this way," says Kay.

"I don't understand any of this." The man looks at no one. The idea that help might exist anywhere at all seems to have left him. With Mr. Kay he goes through the door and together they start down a corridor.

The man says, "What's this place you're taking me to? What did he call it?"

26

"The Black Room."

"Why is it called that?"

"Because it's black." Flatly.

"Painted black? Black walls or what?"

"It's a room. And it's black."

"You're putting me in solitary?"

"You'll be alone."

"What for?"

Kay shrugs. "That's the point of the whole thing."

The man makes a sound something like a titter. "What whole thing?"

Kay looks at him with pity. "You know."

"I *don't* know. That's the whole trouble. I don't *know*."

"You think you don't but you do."

The man shakes his head as though he would clear it, as though it could be cleared. "There's got to be a point to all this," he says.

"Oh, there is."

"You ask for my help—"

"We need your help."

"And I want to give it to you. Whoever you are, I don't care. But I can't make out what you want, what kind of help. It's all double-talk."

"Right now maybe." Kay's voice hints of sympathy.

"You mean I'll understand eventually?"

"It's possible." Then, "Here we are."

There is a door, ordinary, like most doors except

27

that when Kay opens it, it moves heavily on its hinges. The man says, "I can't see a thing in there."

"This is The Black Room."

"Switch on a light."

"There's no light of any kind in The Black Room. Once I close the door nothing will be visible including your hand before your face."

"I'm not going in there!"

"Now now now now," Mr. Kay's voice is still gentle but it is implacable and he puts his hands on the man's arms, holding them firmly. "Don't make a fuss."

"Help, somebody! Help!"

"Cut it out now. I'm going to close the door."

Inside the room there is no sound but the man's breathing which is deep and rapid. "Are you there?" he asks. "Are you there? Mr. Kay, say something if you're there."

"I'm here."

"It's black as hell."

"You haven't got any matches on you by any chance, have you?"

"No."

"Pardon me, I'll just check."

"Don't touch me!"

"I'm not going to hurt you." And he doesn't, just pats the man's clothing all over, fishes in a few pockets and that is all.

"I told you," the man says childishly.

"I know you did." Mr. Kay's voice still sounds benign. Then, more briskly, he says, "Once I go out that door and close it, you'll be in total darkness and total silence. No light and no noise. Except, of course, what noise you make yourself. We can't do anything about that."

"It's nice to know there's something you can't do—"

Mr. Kay breaks in. "You'll be fed. Once a day. Never at the same time."

"How will I know when?"

"It'll be either just before you get hungry or just after you've stopped being hungry."

"You'll bring it to me?"

"You'll find it somewhere on the floor."

"How will I find it if I can't see it?"

"You'll feel around till you come to it. There'll be bread and water and once in a while some cheese or a piece of fruit. If I'm in the mood."

"Look, Mr. Kay—if that's your name—"

"That's what I'm called."

"Will you tell the warden something for me?"

"The who? The warden?"

"Whatever he is. The keeper."

Kay's voice is full of scorn. "Keeper!"

"You know who I mean. The man in charge."

"That's Mr. Zee. The end of the line. Tell him what?"

29

The man's voice is earnest and intense. "Tell him that I—" He stops short.

"That you what?"

"I've forgotten."

"Well that's a good beginning. Keep it up."

"It was very—rather important."

"I doubt that." Mr. Kay opens the heavy door and a trickle of light falls into the room.

The man speaks hurriedly. "Wait a moment—wait—"

"What now?"

"Let me look at the light."

Kay leans against the wall. "Look at it."

"I can't believe it'll just disappear."

"It could come back."

"Oh it will, it will," Then, when there's no response. "It will, won't it?"

"All depends."

"What does it depend on?"

"You, I guess. You and everybody else."

"What kind of an answer is that?"

Kay sighs. A long sigh and deep. Moving energetically he goes through the door and shuts it carefully. A key turns in the lock. Blackness swallows the room. Silence closes in.

"The thing is," the man says quietly, "the thing is not to be frightened. The only thing to fear is fear itself. Who said that? I mean who said it first? Countless people must have said it in times of emergency. I wonder were they afraid while they were saying it, while they were fearing fear."

The man has not moved. In the smothering dark he hears a sudden sound. "What's that?" he whispers. "I hear something. I actually hear. What is it?" He gasps loudly, something like a scream. "It's my heart! My own heart beating! The thing I hear is my own heart!"

In the watery green room, Mr. Kay and Mr. Zee are conversing. Zee says, "How did it go?"

"Very routine."

"Good."

"He fussed a little."

"Oh?"

"I had to step inside with him for a minute."

"No trouble though?"

"He went numb pretty fast."

"He's a believing type."

"He wanted me to give you a message but then he couldn't remember it."

"Typical."

"He thinks you're some kind of a warden. Or a keeper."

"Poor man."

"You know something, Mr. Zee? I didn't much like it inside that room."

"Oh but you knew you were coming out."

"Even so."

"There's a difference. A large difference."

"Who ever dreamed up The Black Room anyway?"

"There's always been a Black Room, far as I know."

"Hell of a place."

"Yes."

"How long'll he last, do you think?"

"Matter of days. Possibly a week or two."

"Then what?"

"He'll go mad. Or die. Or go mad and then die."

Mr. Kay makes clucking noises with his tongue and teeth. "Wonder what he's doing now?"

"Oh—counting by twos. Then by threes. Then by fours. Anything to keep from thinking. That's what they all do."

The man still gasps a little with each breath as he walks around the room, touching the walls with one hand, putting each foot in front of the other with great care. He speaks aloud but just above a whisper.

"Wolcott, Bristol, Forestville, Southington, Plainville, New Britain, Hartford, connection for—for Worcester. Worcester, Springfield, Storrs—" He stops abruptly, mouth open, eyes staring into the deep darkness. "I left out one. Worcester, Springfield—*Providence*! Yes. Providence. How could I have forgotten Providence? *Then* Storrs. Then Lowell. What comes—*what comes after Lowell*?" After a few seconds of blank staring, slack-jawed—"I can't. I can't. No more. I can't." He shakes his head and hits the wall several times with the flat of his hand. Then—"Come on now. None of that. No more 'can'ts'. Go on. Remember things. Like my address, my telephone number. Why—why I can remember my telephone number from the age of six. Forest Glen 5392. Address, two hundred North Elmwood Avenue. There! How about that? But who lived there? Why I did. With my mother and father and my sister. But who were they? Who are they? For that matter, who am I? I mean it. Who am I?"

The man starts his slow walk around the room again, the fingers of one hand lightly touching the wall as before.

"Remember other things. Later things. The hell with train stops. Remember the ocean. The sand. The sounds of the sea. Waves. Winds. Running on the beach, running the whole length of the beach—and the hard wet sand."

The man stops. He stands quite still.

"God! I'm crying! These are my tears rolling down my face and into my mouth. Now wait a minute, let's not have any of that! None of *that*! Remember other things. Yes."

He starts walking again, putting his feet down harder, leaning forward a little as though against a wind. "Remember the house. No, not the house, I'm not ready for the house. Remember the office. No, I can't think about the office. *I can't even think about my own office!* What happened to me? When did it happen? I was standing at the door with Kay. Yes and he said 'Step inside' or something like that—and I did, I stepped inside. What for? Why, to be obliging. Really! Just not to be difficult! Just in order to be—well, *nice*! Thinking if I'm nice they'll be nice. There was a little scuffle, nothing much. He looked for matches and I let him, it seemed not too important. Then I wanted to send a message but I couldn't remember what it was and— Ah! Then! *Then* is when it started, then, when I couldn't think what I'd wanted to say to Mr. Zee, the man in charge. It had left me, gone out of my head, that all-important message washed away, erased. "What *was* it? Even now I can't remember. I'm not even trying to remember. I can't. It's gone, gone for good and I'm left with a mind that's blank. Oh, my God! Oh, merciful God!"

The man makes a sound in his throat as if clearing it. He starts walking again. "School," he says firmly, "yes, school! Uh—Matthew Arnold, English poet, eighteen twenty eight to eighteen eighty eight, something like that, close enough.

> Strew on her roses, roses,
> And never a spray of yew—

Yes—yes, but what comes after? *What comes after?* Whoa now. Quiet down. It's not the end of the world, you know. Or is it? No. It's not. The end may be close but it's not here yet.

> Is it so small a thing
> To have enjoyed the sun?
> To have lived light in the spring?
> To have lived, to have thought, to have done?

"I don't know the rest. There's a lot more but I never learned it. All those years and years and I never bothered to learn it! Well, think of something else, you know lots of poetry. Oh, but I can't, I *can't*! I want to sleep. I'm afraid to sleep. Will I ever sleep? Oh, please let me sleep. And never wake up. Yes."

The man stands still again, again staring sightless but intense into the unyielding dark. Suddenly—from where? From somewhere but where? There is a noise and the man whispers, "What's that? I heard something." Then again, the tiny high-pitched sound. "I hear it! I hear it! I do hear it! I hear—something! Sshhhh. Quiet. Sshhh." And the man puts a forefinger to his lips. Then he screams. "Aaahhh! It's a rat! They've let a rat in here! I'm shut up with a rat! Help! Help me, somebody!"

Down on his hands and knees now, crawling about the room he goes. "Where is it? Where's the rat? I'll kill it! I'll kill it with my bare hands. Where is it, where is it?" He pounds the floor, violently, randomly. "Where? Where? I can't hear it any more. Where is it hiding? Will it bite? What will it do? Will it—Aaahhhhh!" He screams again, then cuts off the sound abruptly and speaks quietly and deliberately. "That's enough of that. Don't do that again. It does no good, no good at all. Lie down on the floor. Stretch out. Let go. Let what will happen happen. Yes."

Carefully, as though afraid of disturbing or disarranging something, the man eases himself onto the floor. He lies flat on his back; he stretches out his arms, spraddles his legs and, last of all, lets down his head. "Don't fight. Don't struggle. Lie still. Be quiet. Take deep breaths. Don't think. Don't remember. Don't do anything."

The man is very still now. His breathing is slow and even. "It doesn't matter if my eyes are open or closed, isn't that funny? Well not really *funny*. When I go to sleep—if I ever do go to sleep—but of course I will eventually—will my eyes close or stay open? Think about that. I suppose they'll close from force of habit but it really doesn't make any difference here. Now they're open. Yes. Now they're closed. I feel my eyelids raise themselves up, now I feel them come down. But everything stays just the same—black."

The man screams again. "Aaahhhh! The back of my hand! Right there! The rat ran over the back of my hand! Oh my God! But it's here. That's certain, that it's here. Where is it now? I don't hear it. Did I ever hear it or just think I did? Did I really feel it? Oh yes, oh yes I did. I did hear it and I did feel it. I'm not hallucinating, I'm not crazy, not—" And then there is the little treble sound again, repetitive and distinct. "There! I hear it again! And I did feel it on my hand before, I did. Little light feet. Oh why would they do that? Why would they put me in a black room with a rat? They must be devils or the cruelest kind of human beings. Yet I keep thinking they seemed kind. Yes, kind. In an ordinary sort of way but still kind."

The man lies quite still, only his breast rising and falling with his long even breaths. "Where is the rat now? Ssshhh. Wait till it makes a noise. Ssshhh. Wait. It will do something, just wait. Ah! Again! It ran across my hand again! Hold on now. Stay calm. It's not so bad. The rat didn't bite you. No. He simply ran across the back of your hand, that's all. You're not hurt. You're perfectly all right. Perfectly. Perfectly all right."

Now there is the tiny self-contained squeaking sound again, breaking the silence insistently. The man is even quieter now and speaks more quietly. "You don't sound like such a big rat. You sound like kind of a very small rat. Why did I jump at the idea you were a rat? You could be a mouse."

He speaks slowly and thoughtfully. "Couldn't you? A very small little mouse. Why not? And if I should lie here quietly, with my arms spread out like this, would you run across my hand again? I wonder, would you? See? See, I'm calmer now, more relaxed. It wouldn't frighten me now if you were to run across my hand. I think if I stayed very still, very relaxed, I could tell if you were a rat or a mouse. I'm lying very still now. Will you come to me? Will you, whatever you are?"

Something like a smile turns up the corners of the man's mouth. His voice is low now with sounds that are reassuring and inviting. "Don't let my heart beat scare you. That isn't anything really. It's just that I'm a frightened man. Your own heart must be beating with a fear like mine. Isn't that so? Really. I mean it. I'm more frightened than you because I've never been in The Black Room before. But I'm not your enemy so don't you be mine."

His breathing is slower now and more even. "I'm waiting," he says. "I'm waiting."

Then he sighs. Relieved. Grateful. "There you are. There you are at last. On my fingers. Such light little feet. So delicate. I think you must be no more than two inches long."

His eyes are open, staring up at nothing and his lips are curved in a small smile. He whispers, "How are you, my friend? My chum. My mouse-friend? My pal. Mister Mouse, how is everything with you? How does it go? Everything okay? Hunky dory? Well, fine. I'm glad of that. As for me—well, I'm managing. Yes, managing so far. I think I can hold out. For a while anyway. At least I'm not alone. Not quite. Not altogether alone."

The greatest horror is to be alone. Man will do anything, endure anything to avoid it. To postpone that crucial moment when, no matter what he does, no matter what he endures, he must face his own essential aloneness—the very last moment of his life.

In the pale green room, Mr. Kay and Mr. Zee are talking.

"So far so good," says Mr. Kay.

"How apt are you. Always armed with the proper cliché."

"Well, it's true."

"All clichés are true. That's why they're clichés."

"That's what we're after, isn't it? The truth?"

"What we're after, my dear Kay, is the final truth. And that will not consist of any cliché composed to date."

"I suppose not."

"You suppose?"

"Well, I'm sure."

"You'd better be sure. If you're not sure, your position as my deputy is precarious."

"Well, I'm sure. I haven't forgotten the point of this whole thing."

"You'd better not."

"The trouble is—"

"There is no trouble."

"Well, the *complication* is that I'm left to do the dirty work while you—"

"You think my part in this project isn't dirty?"

"You just master-mind it." Kay's voice has a tinge of the whine in it.

"Therefore I undertake the dirtiest part of all. What I dream, you do. That's the way it works. It can't work any other way."

"I suppose not."

"Again you suppose."

"I'm sure it can't work any other way."

"Satisfied?" Behind his desk, Mr. Zee stretches his arms and legs. "I myself am never satisfied," he says. "Never. A master mind is never satisfied till it has the last, the definitive answer."

In The Black Room the man is talking too. " 'Wee sleekit cowerin' timorous beastie'—Robert Burns called you that. You are 'wee' and probably 'sleekit' but I don't know that I'd say you 'cower.' You don't shrink or grovel. Maybe you did at first, when I first moved in on your territory but I don't think so. After all, you came to me in the beginning. You made the first move when you ran across my hand. You can say you did it by accident, running about in the darkness, but I'd rather think it was a gesture of some sort, a salutation, a statement even, reminding me 'We're in this together.' I'm being sentimental, maybe maudlin, because I'm very weak now and feeling very helpless. Helplessness is king here in The Black Room and if you are small and fragile and I am a thousand times your size and strength—well, things are reversed now and I am small and fragile and you are strong."

"Sit here on my hand, Mister Mouse, and let me stroke your head. Yes. Yes. Do you like that? The lightest touch, so as not to alarm you. Tell me you like it. Somehow let me know that you do. You don't know how much it would mean to me to know that I was giving some small pleasure to someone. That is one of the chief horrors of being cut off from everyone and everything, there is no one to serve, no one to help, no one to—to amuse! Yes, amuse! To pass the time of day with, to lighten the weight of the hours. That sounds strange perhaps, especially to a mouse who knows nothing of days or hours. But I never knew before how extremely important it is to bring pleasure and comfort and—and *amusement* into other lives."

With his littlest finger the man is stroking the tiny furred head and the mouse is very still.

"Will I ever laugh again?" the man says more to the dark than to the mouse. "That would be too much to expect, I guess. Yes, I know it is. But I don't mind crying any more. I cry a lot now and I don't care. Tears are from God, I think. Tears are

41

one of God's blessings, I believe that and I wish I had known it sooner. There were times in my life when tears would have helped. At school when I thought no one liked me. Till I found out they only thought I was stuck-up, till I developed this habit of smiling, constantly smiling, smiling at everyone, afraid not to smile. When my first child died, I was afraid to cry over that little body, afraid of the disturbance I might create, the sounds that might come out of me, the spectacle I would present to others. Afraid that crying would leave me depleted utterly, unable to do the things that needed to be done, that I'd go beyond being able or competent, that I would dissolve and become nothing, drowned in my tears. Now I know that's not what would have happened, not at all. Here when I weep at the hopelessness of it all, I start to feel it's not quite so hopeless. Why is that? Do you know, Mister Mouse? 'Mice don't cry,' is that what you're saying? Or would like to say? If you thought my question worth a response, something I very much doubt. 'Mice take life as it comes, Mister Man,' you say, 'and death the same way.' But men can't do that, Mouselet, don't you see? Men rebel and struggle, they twist and turn every which way and they suffer! Oh yes! How they suffer! I suppose mice suffer too but they don't tell anyone about it, not even another mouse. Anyway that's how it appears to me. Suffering goes with living. Mice must know that."

"Feeding time."

"So go do it."

"Perhaps this time I'll slip him a piece of cheese, Mr. Zee."

"Those decisions are left entirely up to you, Kay. You know that."

"While you make the big ones. Right?"

"Quite so."

"Who knows? Maybe my decisions could turn out to be big ones in the long run."

"As you say, who knows?"

"They could make the difference between giving in or going on living."

"Hope and despair."

"You could put it that way."

"So get on with your big decision."

"A small piece of cheese. Very small."

"A small inducement to hope."

"Why not?"

"No reason why not. Also no reason why. Either way, get on with it."

The man is on his knees, slapping at the floor close to the walls of The Black Room.

"It's here somewhere. I've stopped being hungry—oh long ago, long long ago. Hunger stopped and misery filled up the gap. But still I go looking for food. It's an elementary instinct, to feed the body. Keep it from disintegrating. I fear disintegration more than I fear death. I suppose because I don't know for sure what death is. It can only come once and then there's no chance to think about it. One is here, one is now, then suddenly one is neither here nor now, lost forever to limitless space and time. Thinking, dreaming, planning, gaining, losing, winning, all are lost and loving too."

The slapping hands stop. "Aha! Here's the plate. And here's the cup! They appear by magic or so it seems. How do they do that? I don't care. They must have all sorts of secret ways of doing things since they seem to have been at this business for a long time. If I last—if the disintegration doesn't set in—or death doesn't make the final move—I'll try to figure it out but right now—here's bread. And this— this is what? Why I do believe it's cheese, a puny piece of cheese! Is Mr. Kay feeling munificent? Or is he merely eccentric? Arbitrary? Does he sit back on his throne, looking profound, and say heavily to himself, 'I think—I think today—I think that to-day I shall give him a piece of cheese.' Yes, I think that must be it. He didn't just add a piece of cheese as an afterthought. Or maybe he did. I don't know. I'll never know. Meanwhile—it's not bad, this piece of cheese. I can taste it. Or I think I can. Mouse-kin? Where are you? I have here in my hand an undeniable piece of cheese. I've eaten half of it or a bit more. Still there are two rather large crumbs left. Do I hear you? You must make some sort of noise for me to know you are near. Here is my hand. You know my hand, you know it well. You know it is always quiet, always stretched out welcoming you. So come."

A sigh that is like a sob comes from the man's throat. "Yes! Oh you are sitting up on my palm. I felt you sit up. Cheese is a word you never heard before, not from me anyway. They left me a piece of cheese this time. I ate most of it but there are some crumbs. I'm putting them in the breast pocket of my shirt. Understand? Oh, try to understand, my mouse. If you get into my pocket, if you could find your way deep down at the bottom you'll find—don't be frightened! Easy now! You know I wouldn't do anything to hurt you, little friend. There! Head first! Down you go! There. There at last. Ah hah! You've found them. You've found the crumbs of cheese. You are eating. Busy busy little jaws are moving at the bottom of my pocket. You are eating and I—I am almost laughing! Almost but not quite laughing because you are so pleased!"

There is a perfunctory knock at the door of the light green room.

"Come in, Kay."

The tall man opens the door, steps through and closes it behind him. All his movements are made cautiously and gravely as though each had been carefully considered and approved beforehand.

45

Zee says, "Sit down. Take a load off your feet."

But Kay still stands, looking thoughtful. "I gave him a piece of cheese. Small piece."

"What for?"

"Just to give him a little—you know, like you said, hope."

"If you want to drag it out—"

"Bread and water, it gets so monotonous."

"I imagine the last thing that concerns him is monotony."

Kay shifts his weight and runs the fingers of one hand through his hair. "Well, it gets monotonous for me too."

"Yes. There's always that."

"Don't you feel it? Same thing? Day in day out?"

"There's always The Quest."

"Yeah but quest for what? We don't even know for what."

"Someday we shall."

"I wonder."

Mr. Zee speaks more briskly now. "You say he's eating well?"

"So far. Every crumb."

"That won't last."

"I guess not."

"Not if he's like the others, it won't. A few more days."

"Stay out of my way, Mister Mouse. Don't let me

hurt you. Maybe he hasn't left it yet. 'Before you're hungry or after you've stopped being hungry,' is what Kay said. Well, I'm never hungry any more but you are. I take a certain pleasure in the thought of you being hungry, as though you were having feelings and sensations for both of us."

The man slaps the floor near the walls cautiously. "There hasn't been any cheese for—for a long time. I can't count days any more." The slapping stops. The man sighs with something like contentment. "Ah! Found it!" Suddenly he is all concentration. "What's this? Why—why it's an apple. Imagine! An apple! I wonder is it red or green or yellow. Perhaps I could tell by the taste." He takes a bite from the apple, bringing his teeth together savagely and chewing solemnly. "Macintosh? Or have I forgotten the taste of apples? I used to know it so well. Back when I was—oh way back when I was living—living my life as though it were mine instead of something thrust upon me to see whether or not I could endure it. Mister Mouse, have you ever tasted an apple? Do you want to try? Why not? Wait till I bite a piece off for you, a tiny, mouse-sized piece."

Daintily the man nibbles at the apple. "Now. You know where it is. Come now. You know. The pocket. I'm sitting here quietly and in the bottom of my pocket is something new, something different. I wish I could hear you, your little feet, your elegant little feet but that's not possible here. Ah! But

47

there's your voice! You could be saying 'Hello' or 'I'm here' or even 'How are you?' Perhaps one day I'll understand what you say in your little piping voice. Oh! You are running up my arm. Yes, you are on my shoulder, sitting up. I think you are wondering how best to attack the pocket this time. That's it. That's *it*! Simply slide down and into it! Oh clever mouse! To go at it from above. How quickly you learn! I feel you move against my chest and I think I have never felt anything so—so comforting."

"I gave him an apple."

"There's simply no end to your imagination, Mr. Kay.

"I thought I would do it."

"If you want to, you can serve him an entire turkey dinner."

"No need to be funny about it."

"I wasn't being funny. Not intentionally."

"You're never funny. Intentionally or otherwise."

"That's as it should be. The Quest is a very serious thing. The most serious thing ever undertaken by man. You know that. Don't you?"

"I guess I do."

Sharply. "You'd better. If you hope to succeed me."

"How did I get here? How did I come to be living in a soundless, lightless room with a friendly mouse? How did I arrive at this place, these circumstances? For that matter how did I arrive at any of the places, any of the circumstances of my life? I planned, yes, I made plans. But things never seemed to work out precisely as I'd planned them. They bore a certain resemblance but that's about all. The marriage—it looked all right but it wasn't quite what I'd meant when I entered into it. The job—it seemed to be a good job. Actually it *was* a good job but not—not quite what I'd had in mind. Not that I know just what I had in mind before getting married or before going to work. But there was an expectation of some sort that was never realized. Disappointment is what I felt. But it all went so fast. Things developed out of the marriage, out of the work, things that needed my attention. So I never quite knew I was disappointed or what I was disappointed in, not till now. The house—it was a good house, it *is* a good house, a nice house but not—not quite—it's always lacking something, always needing something and it's never finished, always lacking, always needing, never quite— Oh! Are you coming out of my pocket now? Had enough, Mister Mouse? We'll save the rest for later. Some vague time in the future, okay? What are you doing now? Are you trying to get inside my shirt? You're pushing your way between the buttons. What for? What do you want? To be close to me? Is that it? Oh be close, be close to me! What was that? What did you do? I felt something, a small pain. There it is again! And again! What can you be doing? Again! Why I think you are pulling out the hairs on my chest! Is that what you are doing, Mister Mouse? Hey! Yes. Yes, you are. Why? Why would you do that? Not to hurt me, I know you would never hurt me. Why? Are you playing? Are you making up a game? Are you telling me that we must have some diversion in our lives? Our dark silent lives? Oh yes. Yes, I think that must be it. You are telling me that it could be worse. There are things we can do, even in our littleness and our helplessness, there is always something, it is never absolutely hopeless. Oh little Mouse! Oh I understand! You are trying to make me laugh!"

"He ate every bit of the apple."

"Fascinating!"

"Even the core."

"Kay, if you want to play the game that way—"

"It's not a game."

"It's a game played for keeps."

"Anyway, there wasn't a scrap left on the plate."

"I wonder how he manages to keep up his appetite."

"Maybe he exercises."

"By this time they usually lose interest in that sort of thing."

"Yeah. After all, what's the point?"

"Hope can't last forever. Sooner or later it dies."

"With this one it looks like it's going to be later."

"But eventually—"

"What makes him hang on?"

"I'd give anything to know."

"It's darn near two weeks."

"Two weeks tomorrow."

"Should I go in after him?"

"Wait a while longer. He can't last."

"You're sure about that?"

"No one ever has."

"It's only breadcrumbs today. Sorry, Mister Mouse. Ordinary breadcrumbs and fresh water. Do you hear me? I'm talking to you. Where are you? Mouse? I have breadcrumbs for you in my pocket. Where are you? Don't frighten me. You're here, aren't you? Are you here? You're not dead, are you? Did I kill you? Could I have killed you by accident? And not known? Killed my only friend? No. I'd rather kill myself than you. I couldn't have done that, I'd have known. Your tiny body with its tiny bones, I would have felt it beneath my feet. Or my hands. Small as it is, I'd have felt it. But then where are you? Why don't you come when I talk to you? Don't you care? Don't you love me?"

The man grabs his head between his hands and pulls it between his knees and rocks his body back and forth. "Good Lord! Listen to me. I am begging for the love of a mouse. I'm without pride, I'm the lowest of the low."

Staring into the blind darkness with blind eyes, the man says, "No. Not so. That is not so. I am the same as any man who finds himself in The Black Room. Not lower, not higher, not better, not worse, simply the same."

He gets up warily, setting his feet down slowly, heel then toe. He moves a little at a time, searching the ground with his feet. His voice is plaintive. His words come without shame, from the heart. "Mister Mouse, come back. Please come back. Can't you hear me? Where have you gone? There's no place to go in this blackness. I can't look for you for fear I might hurt you in some way. Why don't you come to me? I have food for you."

The man stops his slow pace, stands quite still and catches his breath. "God, what a fool I am! You've gone out of the Black Room! Of course! You've escaped! Where? How? There must be a place. You haven't always lived here. You came in at a certain time. Perhaps when I was deposited here and your curiosity enticed you in. And now you've gone out. Gone out where? To what? And how? There must be a place, a little place, a tiny hole just big enough for a mouse to slip through."

Now the man is on his hands and knees again, his fingers feeling all along the baseboard where wall meets floor. He is breathing heavily now and a tremulous little giggle escapes from him.

"Where? Where? You don't live here all the time, whatever made me think you did? The Black Room isn't your only home, not your permanent home, if you have a permanent home and aren't a transient. You wouldn't pick a place like this, no mouse would do that, nobody would do that. No, you came from somewhere else, you must have. There must be a hole somewhere, yes yes yes."

The man's voice grows fiercer and more insistent. "You came through that hole and you've gone out through that hole and I am going to find it! I— am—going—to—find—it!"

"Back to bread and water again."

"Your preoccupation with food, Mr. Kay, always amazes me."

"It's my only contact with the man."

Mr. Zee leans forward, resting his elbows on his desk and his chin on his hands. "You're not supposed to have contact. With him, with anyone in The Black Room ever. After all this time, haven't you grasped that simple concept?"

Mr. Kay moves his feet uncomfortably and his face has a sullen look. "I don't know as I like the concept. It goes against human nature."

Mr. Zee rises slowly, his gaze tightening on the man's face. "We are here to probe human nature, to dig out its secrets, to lay naked its structure. If you have a nature that is even remotely human, you're not fit for this work. You need a nature that's above all that—a superhuman nature."

"Like yours?"

"Like mine."

Mr. Kay is the first to look away. "I'll try—to do better. Feel less."

"See that you do."

"I only said I'll try. Only I don't know how to go about it."

"Detachment. Separation. What most people think of as the scientific mind."

"I don't know anything about science."

"When we have dissected the soul of man, you'll know everything worth knowing. Believe me. It's true."

The man, crouching, says excitedly, "What's this? Is this it? So tiny! So *tiny*! Is it a hole? A hole just big enough for a mouse to slip through? I think so. I think that's what it is. Oh my God! Then on the other side of this hole, there must be—must be something."

The man lies down flat on the floor, inching himself closer and closer to the wall. "Blasted hole is right next to the floor. Well of course, ninny, where would you expect a mouse to put his hole? Six inches higher just for your convenience? It's no bigger than my thumb by the feel of it. I can't get my face up to it!"

The man's feet push against the floor, his buttocks point upward. "Lord! I'll have to stand on my bloody head." He tries to turn his head a little. He succeeds and his temple rests on the floor, his nose digs into it, he twists his face toward the hole. "I must look like a cow trying to scratch her ear. Provided there was someone to look at me. Provided anyone could see me. Oh I can't—it's not—it won't—I can't—yes I can! I can almost—oh help, somebody! I can't get my eye to the hole oh but I can yes yes I can I can!"

He stays quite still in his grotesque position, feet in the air, propped against the wall, face down except for one cheek which turns a little toward the wall, hands on the floor for balance. He whispers to himself in a sort of quiet ecstasy. "I see! Oh I *see*! I see light! I do! I do! A very little little light!" Then in a softer whisper, deep in his throat, "Oh thank you. Thank you. Thanks to whatever, whomever, for this little bit of light."

The man stays in his impossible position for a long time. He seems to be drinking from some hidden spring.

"What's happening now? Where is the light going? Or is it going? It's dim. It's fading. No, not fading but moving away from me. Oh don't go! Don't move! Please stay! Now there's something the other side of the hole, something I've never seen before or not so close. Something—I think it's gray, a dark gray, not quite black but nearly. And it moved! Ever so slightly, it moved! What is it I'm seeing? What can I be looking at?" A little sound, a sort of 'hpppp' escapes from the man and his mouth stays open. "It's my mouse," he whispers, breathing into his words, expelling wonder and admiration with his breath. "He's here! He's on the other side of the hole! I am looking into the small eyes of my friend. And he is looking into mine."

All at once the man's body collapses. Feet and legs and back and shoulders fall to the floor. With his arms he embraces himself and he rolls from side to side. "Oh Lord! Oh Lord Lord! It's too much! Altogether too much!" He takes a few short quick breaths. He lies panting like a dog after a long run, after too much exertion, too much excitement.

Then, quietly, "Who couldn't think of such a thing? Who could think that I—that anyone could be straining at a mouse-hole, bent almost double, to look into the eye of a mouse? It's too much, yes, too much. I can't take it in, I can't believe it happened. Yet I know it happened. It's all that happened and it's everything that happened. I did it because it meant everything. But what did it mean? How did it come about? I can't comprehend it at all. What caused it? What exactly led me to such an effort resulting in such a posture and ending in such a revelation? Oh God! Oh God! I ask you—knowing there's no answer except that a joke is being played on me—a gigantic joke—and even if I fail to catch the precise point of the joke, still I can tell that it is funny, seen in the light of my mundane life, I can see that it's funny and I, always ready, always eager to please, I shall try to laugh."

And starting grudgingly from his chest, climbing to his throat, comes something like a laugh, forced up, forced out, a jagged, rasping sound that little by little grows in volume and in likeness to a sound of amusement and appreciation. Encompassed as he is by blackness, the man is laughing.

In the room painted light green, Mr. Kay says, "He's off his fced."

"Oh?"

"Hardly ate anything the last few days."

"So it's starting."

"What is?"

"The decline. We knew it would sooner or later."

"Think I'll give him a different kind of fruit next time."

"I really don't see why you want to bother."

"Maybe some chesee too."

"Suit yourself."

"Look," says Kay, "the idea was never to starve the poor bastard. If that was the idea, I wouldn't give him anything at all."

"He's beginning to starve himself."

"Can he do that?"

"Stay away from food and water, you'll be gone in a few days."

"No kidding."

"Animals know that."

"Well, I never knew it."

"There's lots of things animals know that men don't know."

"Must be."

"Especially you."

The man is lying on his stomach, his arms pillowing his head. "If I could cry. If God would bless me with tears. But there's a place beyond crying. There's a despair too deep for crying. And that's where I am. In the depths, in the pit of despair where tears will not come. I am simply—there."

He turns over and lies on his back. His eyes that see nothing still stare at nothing. "Crying is for the very young. Children think that their tears will influence someone. That someone will arrive presently and do something. At the very least, come and be there. Maybe say something or make a noise of some sort to show that someone is there. Near."

The man turns on his side. "But grown people know, after a while, that there's nobody. No one will come, no one will make sounds, sounds of comfort, sounds of reassurance, sounds of any kind. No one will stand over the bed, looking down and making sounds."

He pulls his knees almost up to his chin. "Here in the dark, here in the silence, there's nobody. Not a creature is stirring, not even a mouse."

He hugs himself. "I can't laugh. I can't cry and I can't laugh."

Now he flings himself over onto his back.

> They are not long, the weeping and the laugh-
> ter,
>   Love and desire and hate.
> I think they have no portion in us after
>   We pass the gate.

He is silent for a time, his body is quiet. Then, "I can still remember poetry. That's something, I guess. I'm not quite mad as yet, not if I can remember poetry. Anyway I hope I'm not mad. But I think—I think I am about to pass the gate, the gate of sanity, the gate of life."

> They are not long, the days of wine and roses,
>   Out of a misty dream
> Our path emerges for a little while, then closes
>   Within a dream.

The man heaves a long sigh. "I think my life is closing," he says.

Then out of the utter stillness comes the familiar sound, no louder than a fingernail scraping a blackboard.

"Oh. You're back," the man says and the faint sound is repeated.

"You're back, are you? Well, it's too late."

The sound again.

"I have food for you. In the pocket of my shirt. Some crumbs of cheese. And part of a pear."

The squeaking voice is a trifle louder now and more insistent.

"You'll have to come to me if you want it," the man says. "I can't look for you again. I just don't care any more."

We all know it but nobody says it. The drama of life is not played out on the battlefield or even in love affairs. The drama of life—the only real drama— takes place in the dark silent soul of every man or woman who has had the luck—good or bad—to live.

Kay says, "He hasn't eaten a thing for two whole days."

"Oh?"

"The last thing he ate was the pear."

"He's starting down the slide."

"You sound like you enjoy this."

"Well, I don't."

"Then why do it?"

"It's necessary. We need the information. It's the most important information in the world."

"Couldn't we get along without it?"

"Would you want to get along without it?"

"I'm willing to try."

"Well, I'm not."

"I can see that."

"Neither is anybody else."

Kay shifts his weight, frowns. "You could talk to them. They'd listen to you. Make them see it's not absolutely vital."

Zee smiles up at the taller man. "But it *is* vital. You know it's vital. And they know it too."

Kay turns from the desk; his hands flutter in mild exasperation. "I just think maybe it's not worth—all this. Over and over again the same thing."

"It's worth 'all this' and more."

"I don't know," Kay murmurs.

"Look. You're a good fellow and you're not the stupidest man in the world. But there are things that are, let's say, beyond your comprehension. You agree?"

Kay hangs his head like a schoolboy who has done badly, failed a minor test. "I guess so."

"You guess so?" Zee's manner is that of the stern but fair and essentially kindly schoolmaster.

"I—I'm sure. I'm sure there are things that are beyond my comprehension. All the same—" He stops.

"Yes? What were you going to say?"

"How do I know they're not beyond your comprehension too?"

Zee stares at the face above him as though he could not recognize it. His eyes are full of disbelief. Then he turns abruptly to his desk and starts to collect some papers and puts them in a neat pile.

"You just keep on doing your job and don't bother your head with things that don't concern you." He pats his small stack of papers, then swings back and looks up at Kay. "Now. You say he hasn't eaten for two days. How about the water? Has he been drinking any water? That's important because once they become dehydrated the end isn't far off."

In The Black Room the man slumps against the wall, his legs limp and separated, his hands idle in his lap. From somewhere comes the soft, insistent little sound, repeating and repeating.

"I hear you. Oh I hear you. But I don't care. Even if I did care, I'm not sure I'm strong enough to go looking for you."

The man turns his head away from the place where the tiny falsetto voice seems to come from and there is petulance in his voice, a faint exasperation. "There must be food all over the room. Why don't you go look for it? I haven't eaten any of it for—oh, for a long time. So stir yourself and don't always be depending on me."

62

The little sound repeats and repeats and the man sighs deeply. "You really want me to bring it to you, don't you? Play the old pocket game. Well those days are over, my friend." Tears form and roll slowly down the man's cheeks. "I loved you," he says faintly and tears creep into the corners of his mouth. "I loved you, you know that? I thought you loved me. In your own little mousy way. But you didn't. I was just someone to feed you and that's all."

The tears have stopped now and the tired man stares into the dark and his voice is tired too. "Our friendship has come to an end, Mr. Mouse. As all things come to an end."

He clears his throat, dabs at his cheeks and eyes and raises his head a little.

We thank with brief thanksgiving
    Whatever gods may be
That no life lasts forever,
That dead men rise up never,
That even the weariest river
    Winds somewhere safe to sea.

His head sinks onto his chest and he whispers, "Algernon Charles Swinburne, English poet, eighteen thirty-seven to nineteen oh nine."

In the room with walls of lifeless green—
"He isn't drinking any water either."

"Oh that's too bad."

"You feeling sorry for him by any chance?"

"Don't start up with me, Kay."

"It's not like you to go soft."

"I'm not going soft. It's just—just—"

"Just what?"

"I had high hopes for him. That somehow he'd be different. Well, maybe someday I'll learn. Nobody survives The Black Room. Absolutely nobody."

In the blackness, the small falsetto voice persists. Weakly the bass voice answers. "Oh, all right. One more time. One last time I'll look for you."

The man starts searching the angles of the room, his hands slapping feebly. "I don't know why," he whimpers. "It's hard and I don't care any more. But I'll do it. I'll bring you the cheese and the pear. My legacy to you, Mister Mouse. With all my worldly goods I thee endow. My final salute. *Morituri te salutamus.*"

He stops to rest, panting a little. "Where is that little hole of yours, Mister Mouse? I found it once. Where is it? I'd like to see a bit of light before the last darkness closes in."

Once more and more feebly, the man feels along the edges of the wall where it meets the floor. "Is this it? Can this be it? Yes! Yes!" He sits still again. Overcome. Each breath is a long sigh. "I found it. I found it. It was right here. My hand found it. Now. Now to see the light again."

Slowly the man twists his body. His feet rise up. His arms support him though they are trembling. His head pushes up against the wall. "Oh! I'm much too weak. I can't get my eye to it."

His face mostly mashed into the floor, his feet stabbing at the wall to keep a balance with his arms, the man is grotesque. You could call him laughable. "Oh there! There it is! The little morsel of light! The lovely sliver of light!"

Then his feet fall to the floor. Limp, he lies on his back, staring without sight at nothing but faintly smiling. "I'm stronger now," he says. And out of the blackness comes the high piping sound. "I'll find you," he says. "Keep talking. I'll find you." On his hands and knees now, the man crawls slowly around the edges of the room. "I think I'm nearer. Keep talking. I'll find you."

"I can't tell what's going on in there."

"Patience, Mr. Kay."

"He's drinking some water again."

"That's good."

"But no food."

"That's bad."

"I'd like it if he ate a piece of fruit."

"You're such a mother hen."

"It's my job, isn't it? I do what I can to keep them alive."

"Quite so."

Kay's voice is plaintive. "It's not my fault if they—" He turns away.

Zee's voice is sharp and incisive. "Now none of that! The last thing in the world we need is for you to get sentimental. Nothing in the scientific field was ever accomplished through sentimentality. Or anger. Or love. Or pity. Or indignation or outrage or any other emotion. It's 'everlastingly keeping at it,' as my mother used to say."

" 'Sticktoitiveness,' my mother used to say.

"Is it possible we had the same mother?" Zee asks lightly.

Kay looks hard at the man behind the desk. "Not possible," he says, "not even remotely possible."

"You sound very loud," the man whispers. "I must be close. Or has my hearing become sharper? Does the hearing improve when there's nothing to hear? I've read about people who live in the forest and never hear anything louder than the falling of a tree and their hearing is very sharp and never fails them even when they are quite old. What about a man who lives in The Black Room and never hears anything louder than the squeaking of a mouse? What about him?"

The man stops, resting on his haunches, tilting his

head first to one side, then to the other. Out of the dark comes the high tinny sound, urgent and demanding. The man says, "You are very near now, I think. I think I can reach out and touch you."

Then he screams. A long shrill scream and he falls flat with his face burrowing into the floor. Then he rolls over on his back, still screaming and rocking his body from side to side. "Oh no! Oh no! It didn't happen, it didn't happen! I won't believe it happened! I won't believe I reached out my hand and you bit me. I won't believe that, not that, not that you bit my hand when I was going to feed you. I can't believe that, I won't believe that, not that, no!"

He stops rocking and lies quite still. "But it's true." Then he yells into the dark above him. "There's no end to it! No end to the shocks and the suffering and the cruelty and the horror, no end to it. When you think you've borne it all, there's more. And more. And more."

Mr. Kay knocks on the door with the insipid green walls. When he hears Mr. Zee's voice say "Yes?" he turns the knob slowly, slowly enters and walks slowly to the desk.

"How is he?" Zee asks.

"Not eating. Not drinking."

"I see."

"I think myself it's time to go in."

"You think he's alive?"

"He could be, I guess."

"In his right mind?"

Kay looks down at the man behind the desk with something like contempt. "You trying to be funny?"

"I merely asked."

"Why don't you try The Black Room yourself sometime?"

"I may have to."

"Don't kid me. You wouldn't do it."

"If I have to I will."

"You think you could stick it out?"

"For a time."

"How long?"

"That remains to be seen."

"Three weeks?"

"It would depend on my resources, wouldn't it?"

"I guess that's what it always depends on."

"Quite so. One thing I'm sure of. You wouldn't last a day."

"No end to it. No end ever. It goes on and on and there's no end to it." The man is sitting quietly, leaning against the wall, his hands still and helpless in his lap. He turns his head a little when he hears the insistent squeaking. "Why did you bite me?" he says, "Why is the name of Heaven would you bite me? I meant you no harm. I've never done you any harm so why would you turn on me and bite me?"

He leans a little toward the squeaking sound. "Explain it to me. Because I need to know. I need to know this one thing before I die. It's important to me for reasons I do not comprehend and therefore cannot explain. Look. Look if you can, if mouse eyes can see in the pitch blackness. Here's what I brought you. Three little pieces of cheese. I'll put them down here. You'll find them. Probably after I'm dead. And a piece of pear. It's warm now and mashed to a pulp. But I'll put it in between the pieces of cheese. Do you want to bite me again? Go ahead. I don't care. No more. You know what? I could kill you if I wanted to. I have the strength for that. I think I do. But I don't want to. For a little while you kept me from going mad. And for that I'm grateful. So go on. Bite me if you want to. Go ahead."

Mr. Kay says, "I really think I should go in."

"You said that before."

"Now I'm sure of it."

"You have my permission."

"Thanks a lot."

"I always leave the final judgment up to you."

"Well that's my final judgment. That I should go in after him."

"All right."

"I want to do it. And I hate to do it."

"Why is that?"

69

"I hate to think of what I'll find. However—"

"Yes?"

"I'll hate it worse tomorrow." Kay starts to go.

"Oh Mr. Kay—"

"Yes?"

"If, by any chance, the man should be alive and if he should be even remotely in his right mind—"

"Not likely."

"No. But if he should be, take him upstairs and let him take a shower. Let him shave. Give him some clean clothes. Then bring him down here to me."

"That's *if* he's alive and in his right mind."

"There's always that chance. There's always been that chance."

In The Black Room the man still sits quietly, listlessly, leaning against the wall. His head shakes a little. "You're not saying anything, Mister Mouse. Are you still here? Or did you run away? Did you run to your mouse-hole? Did you run through to the other side to live in the light, in the beautiful light? Or are you still here?" The man's hand searches the floor apathetically. "Why don't you say something? Don't you have one final word for me? Of any kind at all? No last little squeak? I won't be here much longer, Mister Mouse, or if I'm here I'll be too deranged to acknowledge what once was our friendship."

The man's groping hand comes suddenly to rest.

It trembles a little as does his whole body. "What's this?" he whispers. "Is it you? Is this your furry little body? I think—yes—no—what is it? What am I touching? So small—so— Oh no! It can't be. One—two—three—four—"

The man gasps several times. His hand does not move. His heavy spasmodic breathing is the only sound in The Black Room. Then he emits a sort of soft cackle, short and staccato. "Why— Why you're not Mister Mouse. You're Missus Mouse. You're Mother Mouse. Four—five babies. You were afraid I might hurt them. That's why you bit my hand. Yes, yes, I understand. But now you trust me. Now you know. Oh Mother Mouse! Oh my beautiful little Mother Mouse! My dear, my own. My sweet one, my dearest friend, my only—oh! tears again! I'm crying again. God has blessed me again. Mother Mouse, I am crying and my tears are falling on my hands and on you and on your children."

There is a sound near where the weeping man sits but he does not look up. The heavy door opens and a slice of light falls into the room. It filters through the man's tears and into his eyes. He blinks.

"You there?" asks Mr. Kay.

"What?"

"I think I hear you. You there?"

"What?"

"I came to get you."

"Oh."

71

"You can find your way to the door, can't you?"

"Yes."

"Well, come on."

The man crawls to the door, squinting at the light though it is not strong. Mr. Kay helps him to his feet and holds him as he starts to sway a little.

"Okay, are you?"

"Okay."

The two men, one supporting the other with something like tenderness move out of The Black Room and into the lighted corridor.

"Down this way," says Kay.

"Where to?"

"You'll see. You'll like it."

"I will?"

"A lot. It's nice."

"Okay."

"Now, right here—on your right there's some stairs. Can you see 'em okay?"

"I see."

"Well good. Good. That's fine. After all that time I thought maybe—well, the hell with *that*. Now get hold of the railing with your left hand. I'll be on the other side of you and I'll help."

"I can do it."

"I don't want you to fall."

"I can do it by myself."

"All right. Okay. Take your time. No rush."

Slowly, heavily, the man climbs the stairs.

"You okay?"

"Okay."

"You look to be in pretty good shape. You were off your feed there for a while and I started to worry."

"That so?"

"Couldn't help myself. Mr. Zee thinks I take things too personally but that's the way I am. I put myself in the other guy's place."

"Very interesting."

They have reached the top of the stairs.

"Straight ahead," says Kay.

"Where are we?"

"You'll see. Right behind this door." Kay pushes a door open and a brilliant light shines out. The man cringes.

"Too bright for you?"

"I'll get used to it."

"Sure you will. This is the dressing room. Where we get you fixed up."

"I see."

"First you take your clothes off. Then you take a shower. Unless you'd rather have a tub."

"Shower's fine." The man takes off his shoes and socks, then his slacks.

"Give 'em to me. I'll fold 'em up. I got new ones for you."

"Okay."

"Here's a razor and shaving soap."

"Fine."

"Bet it'll be good to get that beard off, huh?"

"Yes." The man stares at his face in the mirror over the washbowl.

"You haven't changed much."

"No?"

"Not that I can see. When you're finished shaving, I'll turn on your shower. How do you like it? Hot, cold or in between?"

"In between."

"Right."

In the green room belowstairs, Mr. Zee paces the floor. "I should know by now. Did he make it or didn't he? If he didn't, Kay would have sent word that it was over. Another failure. Or if he was in bad shape—he'd have asked me what to do with him. So it must mean—at the very least it means he's alive. All that remains is to find out if he's sane, how much damage has been done. If he's sane, how sane? Is the damage irreparable? How to repair it? No simple therapy will work if he's psychotic, I know that. Deep analysis—he couldn't take that if he's badly traumatized. Then what?" Zee punches one fist into the palm of the other hand. "He must have come through in some kind of shape. Will I be able to talk to him? Will he be able to formulate answers? Will he be able to reflect on what's transpired and grasp the significance of the whole experiment?"

Upstairs the man steps out of the shower and Kay hands him a towel. "How'd it feel? Good huh? Water hot enough for you?"

The man nods and starts to dry himself.

Kay goes on. "Nothing like a shave and a shower, am I right?" He looks at the man appreciatively. "I think you've lost a little weight. Few pounds. Oh. Here. I bought you some socks. Hope they're the right size. Maybe I should have asked you your size before you went in there but to tell you the honest truth I never thought you'd come out."

The man glances sharply at Kay. "Was that the idea?"

"No no. Not at all. Not necessarily anyhow. Yeah. I think you've lost about five pounds. That's not bad. Care to weigh yourself? There's some scales over there."

"No thank you."

"The rations were pretty thin, I know that. But you weren't putting out much in the way of energy. Or did you do exercises in there?"

"No."

"How did you like the fruit I left you? And the cheese. Did you like it?"

"Very much."

"I thought you would. Mr. Zee couldn't see the point but I said heck! Break the monotony. Was I right?"

"What?" The man reaches for his shirt but Kay

stops him. "Hey! Don't put that shirt back on. I brought you a clean one. I think it'll fit."

"Thank you."

"Give me your old one and I'll throw it out."

"Don't touch it."

"What?"

"Keep your hands off that shirt."

"You want it? It's pretty dirty."

"I want it."

"I'll wash it for you."

"Leave it alone."

"You want it the way it is?"

"Just the way it is."

"If you say so. Well? Are you ready?"

"Yes."

"So let's go see Mr. Zee. He's dying to talk to you."

In the pallid green room, the short, stout Mr. Zee pours himself a drink of brandy. "Just one won't hurt. I never get drunk. I always maintain sufficient—sufficient sobriety to command the situation and write a proper report. And I will this time. But the prospect of—of talking to a man who's just come out intact—it's too much for me. A drink won't hurt. Even two." He fills the small glass again. "It's exciting. Terribly exciting. It could be a breakthrough. After all our trouble, keeping our eyes on the desired end—" he swallows the brandy convulsively. "I can hardly believe—I hardly dare believe—"

Outside the door to the green room Kay stops. "You mind?" he says to the man. "Mind waiting here a minute? While I talk to Mr. Zee? It won't take long."

The man nods without speaking. Kay pats him gently on the shoulder, almost fraternally. He knocks on the door and with a quick, parting smile at the man, opens it and enters and closes the door behind him.

"Well!" he says. "Drinking so early?"

"How is he?" Zee puts the glass down heavily on the desk.

"First time I've ever seen you take a drink in this office."

"Cut the talk. How is he?"

"Well, you'd be surprised."

"Damn it to hell, how is he?"

"Alive."

"I assumed that when you didn't come right back."

"Lost a few pounds."

"Naturally."

"He's pale."

"Damn you, how is he?"

There is a wait while Kay walks slowly to the

desk. He perches on the edge of it, drums his fingers on its surface and says, "He's okay."

"Really all right?"

"I told you. He's okay."

"You mean that?"

"No signs of having gone off the deep end. No signs at all. None that I could see."

"You've been with him ever since he came out?"

"All the time. He showered and put on clean clothes and we came down here. He's waiting outside."

"And he's all right? I can talk to him?"

"He's not much of a talker right now but he's okay."

Mr. Zee exhales a long breath. "Ask him to come in."

"Right." Kay goes to the door and opens it. "Will you be good enough to step inside?"

The man inclines his head and steps through the door into the green room.

Zee says, "Mr. Kay, will you wait outside? Please?"

The door closes behind Kay.

"Would you care for a brandy?"

"No thank you."

"Do sit down."

The man looks with mild surprise at Mr. Zee who says, "Take my chair." The man moves slowly to the chair behind the desk. Zee stands, his hands clasped behind his back, a tentative smile mingling with an expression of worry on his face. He says, "You look rather well. Surprisingly well." When the man says nothing, Zee adds, "I'm glad to see you."

"Are you really?"

"Really. Very glad. You've no idea how glad. It's been—let's see—twenty-six days. That's remarkable. Truly remarkable."

Still the man says nothing and Zee goes on. "Uh—tell me something if you can. How does a man survive twenty-six days in The Black Room?"

The man stares at Zee across the desk but does not speak.

"Can you tell me? I really want to know. What does a man need to come out of there intact?"

The man blinks several times and purses his lips. His eyes seem focused on Zee's face but at the same time seem to be looking through and beyond him. "He needs—he needs to care for some living soul."

Zee stares back at the man. There is a silence in the room. Zee says, "That's all he needs?"

"He needs to care a lot."

"That's all? Just that?"

"That. And a little light."

There is another silence. Then Mr. Zee looks down tenderly at the man and speaks softly. "You're very tired, aren't you?"

"Yes," the man says.

"It's been quite an ordeal."

79

"Oh, yes."

"We'd like to give you a complete physical examination, if you don't mind, before you go."

"I can go?"

"Also psychiatric testing."

"Then I can go?"

"One other thing."

Warily the man says, "And what is that?"

"After we've completed both examinations, would you be kind enough to address a few words to the membership? Not a long speech, we wouldn't expect that. But if you'd expand a little on what you've just told me here—"

"Wait a minute—what membership?"

"Don't you know?"

"How am I supposed to know?"

"I thought you'd guessed."

"Is this a club? Some kind of a cult?"

"Not precisely a club. Certainly not a cult."

"Then what is it? Who are the members?"

"People in trouble. Troubled people."

"But—that's practically everybody."

"Quite so. Yes." Mr. Zee looks wistfully at the man. "Will you talk to them, sir? They'd be ever so grateful. Then you can go home."

THE BLACK ROOM

* * * * * * * *

Where do you live? Main Street? Lake Shore Drive? Mulberry Lane? Park Place? Lenox Avenue? Corner of Fourth and Walnut? Three miles out on Route Seven? Come now. You know better than that. You may hang your hat anywhere at all but you live in The Black Room of your own mind.

The Only Blood

Sam Dann

What did we do before we had Radar? The answer is simple. We had women. True, we still have women—ah, but not like the women we had back in what might be called, less complex times. In those days, women seemed to have antennae that were constantly tuned into the moods of their men. Today's women claim they have more important matters to occupy their attention. Perhaps, they do. At any rate, there are very few women around nowadays like Anna-Maria Boda, may she rest in peace in the bosom of the Saints. For the twenty-five years of her married life, Anna-Maria's sensory system had been directed exclusively at the psyche of her husband, Anthony. His needs, his moods, his sorrows, and joys echoed in her brain at almost the exact split second they originated in his. Of course, Anthony was aware of her sensitivity which he referred to as "that spooky business!" Therefore, whenever she asked him a particularly unsettling question, he made little or no attempt to evade the issue.

"You're not hungry tonight, Anthony!"

"Look. I finished my plate."

She shook her head. "You didn't ask for more. It's that ten dollars again."

He nodded slowly. He didn't want her involved. He had managed a good mood all through the meal. How did she find him out? That spooky business, obviously!

"Another ten dollars is missing?" she asked.

"Yes," he answered, "It's missing again."

She sighed. "Can you be sure?"

"Of course, I'm sure!" he answered impatiently. "Don't we have the cash register in the store!"

She shrugged her shoulders. "The cash register—Oh, that cash register! Why do you need a cash register!"

"Because," said Anthony, "That's the way things are done in America."

"Ah!" the note of triumph rang in her voice, "But when you just kept the money in the drawer, *nothing* was ever missing!"

It was an argument he knew he would never win even though all the logic in the world was on his side. "When I kept the money in the drawer, I never knew exactly. This way, everytime you take in money, it prints on a paper. At the end of the day, the machine tells you how much money you should have. To the penny."

As usual, she was not impressed. "Then the machine is wrong."

"That's impossible."

"A machine has no soul," she said. "Therefore, it has no conscience. In which case, it can lie and cheat."

"Please," he exclaimed, "Talk like an American!"

"It's the only thing I cannot understand about America," she went on. "In the Old Country, ignorant people were afraid of devils. Here, smart people are scared of machines."

He threw up his hands. "Why did I marry you? Because I thought you were an intelligent woman!"

"Oh, no! No, no," she said. "You married me because I had a narrow waist and long legs. I had a nice bust, also."

"Anna-Maria!" he protested.

"Well," she reflected, "that might not have been too important. But the slender waist and the slim legs, absolutely! You wanted to be sure your wife would not be a fat, old lady at fifty. And I'm not."

"Anna-Maria," he tried to interrupt, but there was no stopping her.

"But intelligent? No. Never," she insisted. "You would have run away from me if you had even suspected I was intelligent. But how could you dream I was smart? I was too pretty."

"One thing you never were," he said. "And that was modest."

"And why did I marry you?" she asked. "Because you were handsome. And you still are."

He tapped his head. "Even if I'm bald?"

"Oh, yes. It gives you dignity."

He sighed. "I could have made a mistake. Maybe I gave out too much change."

"We're back with that infernal machine, I see," said Anna-Maria.

"Ah, forget it," he declared. "And I'm not even sure the money is missing!"

She smiled. "All right. Let's talk about something else."

"You talk too much as it is," he said.

She laughed. "But this is *your* America! Here, it's not like the Old Country where the man sits fat at the table—the Lord. And the woman stands shaking behind him—the Slave."

"What troubles me," he said, "Is that it's always ten dollars. And it's always on a Friday night. And it's always after ..." He stopped short. She waited for him to continue but he stood up from the table. "I'll go downstairs and smoke my pipe," he said.

She kept her voice very steady. "It's always after ... what, Anthony?"

He shook his head. "Nothing." He took the pipe from his pocket and began to fill it from the pouch. "I wasn't going to say anything."

Her voice was low but the words very distinct. "And, it's always after Louis has been alone in the store. Is that what you wanted to say? Is it?"

It was exactly what he had wanted to say! That spooky business of hers again! He should have known better. What could he hide from her?

"Anthony," she said sadly. "Your own son."

He bit his lip. "I don't know. Louis and I, we're the only ones who touch the money. . . ."

She refused to let him say the rest. "Your *only* son!"

"He's twenty years old," said Anthony. "He wants to be married. Maybe he feels he needs the money to start a house of his own."

"And, therefore," she said scornfully, "he would steal from his own father!"

"I don't know what to think," exclaimed Anthony.

"I can trace my family back five hundred years," she said, proudly. "We have no thieves. Your family, of course, I cannot vouch for."

"Well," he said, "I don't know what to do."

"I could tell you what to do," she offered. "Throw away that machine."

Anthony Boda waited on the corner of the narrow, crowded street. The traffic light was red. Of course, he could have threaded a path between the slow-moving cars and trucks the way most people did. However that would have been against the law. Never mind, they all claimed it was a minor law. How could there be such a thing as a *minor* law? If the law of the land says you may only cross the street when the light is green for you, then that law is just as important as the law that says you must not rob or kill your fellow man, no? Of course! Clearly, it's a dangerous business, this, of letting people decide which laws they should follow and which they could break. Once a thing like that starts, there's no telling where it would end. Yes, there is. It would end where it all began—back in the Old Country—where the richer you were, the more laws you could defy; which meant that, for the very rich, there was no law at all. This was something they never stopped to think about, all the neighbors and friends, but it was the real reason they had left the Old Country, in the first place. Of course, many had never left it. Oh, the bodies were here, but where were the spirits? Day and night, the endless talk of the past. How the air was like wine! How the wine made the blood bubble! Agreed. Here the air was foul but it was breathed by men who were free. And, if the wine was sour, at least, the living was sweet. Where were the famines, the plagues, the depradations of arrogant nobles and insolent bandits? Not here! Never here in America! Why did so many of them behave as if they had never left home? In the Old Country, men would scarcely budge from the village of their birth.

When they came here, they would hardly ever stir from the neighborhood. Eat, work, sleep, die. Discover America, he would exhort them. Go to the night school, the settlement house! Become an American! It's Anthony Boda talking, they said. Anthony, the crazy American.

The light turned green. He walked across the street. As usual, he paused before the entrance to the shop. Surely, it was no longer a novelty, but he always liked to savor the neat, gilt letters: "Anthony Boda and Son Shoe Repairs." The sign man had suggested "Expert Shoe Repairs" but Anthony had refused. Expert, he tried to explain should be a word that existed in the mind of a customer, not on the window of a shop. Naturally, the man didn't understand him. At twenty-five cents a letter, he thought Anthony was only trying to save a dollar and a half. Anthony shook his head sadly. It is the fate of some men to be misunderstood in this world. And then, he smiled. At least, in America, they didn't burn you at the stake for it. He opened the door. A little silver bell tinkled. At the sound, Louis looked up from his work.

"Everything OK, Louis?"

"Yes, Poppa."

Louis at twenty. A little too thin, a bit too serious, but very much the handsome image of a handsome father. One thing you had to say about the Bodas—they were good-looking people. And Anna-Maria's folk could hardly be considered ugly so it was no wonder that Louis was the finest looking boy in the neighborhood. It was true the girls refused to leave him alone—which was probably why he thought he needed more money ... But, here, Anthony felt a sudden shame. This boy, so devoted, so polite, so hard-working, had made Anthony the envy of every father on the block. There had to be another explanation for the missing ten dollars. There simply had to be!

"Time for you to go home, Louis," he said.

"I promised a lady she could have her shoes one o'clock, Poppa."

"I'll finish for you," Anthony said. "Go. Momma doesn't like it when anyone's late to eat dinner."

Louis smiled. "In America, it's called lunch, Poppa."

"Is it?" Anthony asked. "So when do you eat dinner?"

"Six o'clock."

"Then when do you eat supper, Louis?"

"Midnight. After the theater."

"What do the working people do?" Anthony asked. "They're all asleep."

"I guess they just have to miss a meal, Poppa."

"Well," said Anthony, "Even in America, only the rich can afford to eat four times a day."

"Not according to the papers, Poppa," Louis said.

"The rich eat less than the poor. They're always going on diets."

"Didn't I always tell you? It's a fantastic country!"

The bell tinkled. The door opened. A loud voice called out, "Hya, Louie, Old Pal!"

The man who came in was about thirty years old. Although, he appeared heavy, his weight seemed to consist of solid beef rather than fat. There was a wide smile on his face, and he might have given the impression of being good-natured if it hadn't been for his eyes. They were small and dull. Nothing seemed to shine in them. His laugh was cheerful, his voice was agreeable, his manner was breezy—but his eyes were chilling. At the sight of him, Louis became apprehensive.

"What can I do for you, Chuck?" he asked.

"You gotta hand over a fin," said Chuck.

"Uh, Chuck," said Louis, "could we talk about this later?"

"Later?" asked Chuck, "What's later? I'm here now, ain't I? A fin. Get it up." The smile was becoming thinner.

"Louis," Anthony asked. "Who is this man? What does he want?"

"Poppa," said Louis hastily, "It's just a personal thing!"

"Hey, Louie! No reason you shouldn't introduce me to your Old Gent!" said Chuck. "The Association likes to know all its customers! Whaddya say, Pop!"

Anthony looked closely at Chuck. "What Association is this?"

"Listen, Poppa," said Louis. "I can explain everything later!" To Chuck. "I saw you last night. Friday."

Chuck placed a friendly arm around Louis' shoulder.

"I know ya did, Kid. But the executive board had a meet this morning. And you know how prices are just goin' up sky-high all over. Like for instance, Mr. Boda, whatcha payin' for leather alone today? Don't tell me! It's gotta be a fortune! You see what I mean? So what with overhead and everything else, we simply gotta go from ten to fifteen. So hand it over, Louie."

Louis' hand slowly reached for the register. Then, quickly he struck a button. A bell rang. The drawer slid open. He found a five dollar bill and handed it silently to Chuck.

"Louis!" Anthony's voice was angry. "What are you doing!"

"Poppa, please!" Louis' voice begged him.

Chuck's grin widened. He poked a playful finger at Anthony's belly. "Keep smilin', Pop! Everybody smiles today. Lookit this fiver here. Even Lincoln's smilin'! Shows ya done a good thing. See ya next

94

week—same time, same station!" He pocketed the bill, winked and was out the door.

Anthony Boda said nothing. He sat down in his chair. He looked thoughtfully at his son. "So," he said finally, "This is where the ten dollars a week goes. And now, I see it's become fifteen."

"Poppa, I was hoping you ... you wouldn't notice . . ."

"Ten dollars? I wouldn't notice?"

"Some weeks, I was able to pay it out of my own pocket."

"So," said Anthony Boda. "We now belong to an Association." He paused he considered the statement. "For what reason?"

"Because we have to," Louis answered.

"We have to?" Anthony's voice was calm. His face was becoming dark.

"Poppa! *Everybody* belongs! Every shop on the street! Every store in the neighborhood!"

Anthony Boda rose angrily to his feet. "My son, it's quite possible you have forgotten who you are! Let me remind you! You are not a sheep who follows! You are a man who leads!"

"Poppa, Poppa, you don't understand."

"Oh, I understand," said Anthony, "didn't we have these bandits in the Old Country? One of them rode up to our farm. Your grandfather shot him out of the saddle!"

"Yes, Poppa," said Louis. "And the next day, my

grandfather was dead with fifty bullets in his back."

"Yes, that's right! In the back! The cowardly scum were afraid to face him!"

"But he was dead, Poppa!" It was almost a cry of agony from Louis. "He was dead, don't you understand!"

Anthony's voice was calm, even gentle. "I understand that was the Old Country, my son. But this is America, where no man can be forced to live on his knees. Here, men will fight. And I will lead them."

"Lead who, Poppa?" Louis asked, "Lead who?"

"Stay here a few more minutes, Louis," said Anthony. "This should not take long."

Anthony Boda opened the door and walked out of the shop. For a moment, he stood in the middle of the sidewalk. Louis' question still rang in his ears: "Lead who? Who?" Anthony smiled. There was so much the boy didn't know. Every store on the block was owned by a man who had left Europe to escape the bandits. For the bandits had overrun almost the entire continent. A bandit named Mussolini now held all of Italy in tribute. Another robber chief, Hitler, had enslaved the Germans. Fat, little Franco in Spain, evil-eyed Stalin in Russia, each and every one a bandit who kept millions in bondage. And who were they, what were they, for the most part, in the beginning? Petty hoodlums like Chuck! Yes. The men in this neighborhood would handle Chuck. He entered Vito's Grocery next door. Vito, a burly six feet, two-hundred-and-fifty-pound mountain, who had never turned his back on a fight, stood in the midst of his redolent cheeses, delicious meats, and fragrant spices. He was slicing a ham. His eyes lighted up at the sight of Anthony Boda.

"Hey, Mr. America!" But there was a word of good-nature in his voice. He offered a chunk of ham to Anthony.

"Thank you, Vito," said Anthony.

"You wanna whole san'wich, Tone?"

"No. I just had my dinner."

"So how's everything, Tone?" asked Vito.

"Not bad," Anthony answered.

"Tell me," said Vito, "You like the ham? I bought it off a new guy. Whaddya think?"

"Not enough salt."

"Not enough salt," Vito echoed. "But wit' some people, it's too much salt. Ah, whaddya gonna do? Can you please everybody?"

"Never," said Anthony.

"Listen, Tone. I'm havin' a little trouble wit' the oldest. You know, Gino."

"Gino's a good boy," said Anthony.

"Good boy? He don't wanna work! Listen, Tone, I see Louis ina shop every day. How'd ya get him to do that?"

"I ask him," said Anthony.

"You ask him? I ask Gino. I tell him I'll bust his head if he don't come in here an' do a day's work. Ah! But it don't do no good. I take off the strap, his Momma starts to cry, and all we get is hollerin' and screamin' an' I can't stand it!"

"Why don't you ask him to come in because you need him, Vito?"

"Listen, Tone—you wanna do me a big favor. Gino, he likes you."

"And I like Gino," said Anthony.

"You wanna talk to Gino? You know what I mean?"

"I think so." said Anthony.

"Thanks, Tone. I feel better already. Anytime I can do you a favor, you just lemme know. You promise?"

"I promise. Vito, you know somebody named Chuck?"

"Chuck?" Vito's eyes narrowed. "Chuck Who? Chuck What?"

"A bandit who thinks that this is the Old Country," said Anthony.

Vito picked up a rag and began to wipe the counter industriously.

"I don't know nobody called Chuck," he said.

"And you're not paying Chuck fifteen dollars a week for dues?"

Evidently, Vito had discovered a stubborn stain on the counter. He rubbed at it furiously.

"Are you telling me you don't belong to the Association, Vito?"

Vito threw the rag down on the counter. "What th' hell dya want from me, Tone!" his voice was becoming angry.

"America has been very good to us, Vito—to you and to me," said Anthony.

"Whaddya startin' up wit' America again for! OK! I salute the flag, I kiss the floor! Whaddya want me do!" the anger was starting to build.

"We have to fight for America, Vito," said Anthony.

"Ya mean, there's a war on! OK! I'd enlist, I swear to God! But I got a wife! Six kids! I'm cross-eyed and I gotta bad back! Nobody would even take me ina Army! What I'll do if there's a war, I'll get a job in a factory like my uncle did last time! An' he made a fortune!"

"Vito, it's a different kind of war," Anthony said. "This thing—this business of tribute—this is not American. You understand. This is Old Country. We must not let it take root here. Flourish here. We must stamp it out. It's your duty, Vito."

Now Vito tried to keep his anger under control.

"My duty," he said, "is to keep my mout' shut and my nose clean because that's my duty to my family."

"Are you afraid, Vito?" Anthony asked.

"Tone, you and me, we been friends thirty years."

"Are you afraid, Vito?"

Vito clenched his fist. "I never thought I'd see

th' day I'd punch you ina nose!" He was starting to breathe hard.

"You better get outta here!"

"You should be punching somebody's nose," Anthony said. "But not mine."

"I don't wanna talk about it, Tone."

"Why not?"

"Because I don' wanna talk about it!"

"I know you're scared Vito," said Anthony.

"Tone, there's nothin' we can do about this thing, so just forget it, an' 'at's all!"

"If we all stand together," said Anthony.

"Go stand someplace else!"

"Vito, is this you talking?"

"Now, you better get outta here, Tone, an' I ain't kiddin'"

"Vito, I'm asking you to . . ."

But Vito would not let him finish. "Get outta here!" he shouted furiously. "I said get outta here! Goddam Agitator! Get outta here!"

Could he have been wrong about Vito all these years? Was the man basically a coward at heart? The hell with him! There were other men—men who would not be pushed around. Enrico, who owned the fruit and vegetable store; quick-tempered, quarrelsome, constantly spoiling for a fight. There could be enough of a fight here to satisfy even Enrico's appetite. And Gus, the Plumber. Mario, the hardware man. And Hymie Markowitz, the tailor. Hymie was always talking about the dignity of man. And how anyone who sought to destroy it, must be fought tooth and nail—"smite them hip and thigh" was how he put it. Well, here was some fighting and smiting for Hymie, and right in his own backyard, too. Quickly, he compiled a list of fighters in his head. Soon, he would collect an army, an invincible army. And the bandits would be wiped off the face of the earth.

Anthony Boda, crusader! He was not the first, nor would he be the last to discover that crusading can be a lonely affair. And very often, your crusader chief comprises the entire personnel of the army. An hour later, he walked slowly into Vincent's Restaurant. Vincent, himself, was sitting at a rear table, going over his bills, a bottle of wine in front of him. Tony sat down. Without a word, Vincent poured him a glass.

"Is this the new wine?" Anthony asked. Vincent nodded. Anthony sipped.

"Well?" Vincent wanted to know.

"It's just a little bit . . . sweet," ventured Anthony.

"Somebody else told me it was a little bit sour," said Vincent. "Well, Tony. . . ?"

"Well, Vincent?"

"I asked you first," said Vincent.

"I'll tell you," said Anthony. "You learn something every day."

"And what did you learn today, Tony?" asked Vincent.

Anthony drained his glass. He wiped his lips. He seemed to think for a moment. Then he said, "I learned that men who appeared to be strong, proud, honest—are afraid to join their hands together."

"Yes, I heard about that, Tony," Vincent said.

"What did you hear?"

"Oh," said Vincent, "You been going into every shop on the street to get people to fight the Association."

Anthony slammed the table with his fist. "If we all joined hands, we could crush those vermin!"

Vincent sighed. "You went from place to place," he said, "And everybody turned you down, right, Tony?"

Anthony shrugged. "It wasn't so much they turned me down—but the terror in everybody's eyes. Mother of God, Vincent! Did they come to America to live on their knees! Ah, the hell with 'em! You and me, Vincent. The two of us. We will be enough for the job."

"Are you asking me to join you?"

"Well, sure, I'm asking, Vincent!"

"Anthony," Vincent said. "I will also turn you down."

"You!" Anthony could hardly keep the incredulity from his tone. "You will not. . . ! What are you telling me, Vincent!"

"Tony, these are not just a pack of street wolves. They work for a powerful, important person."

"You can live like this, Vincent?" Anthony asked.

"A person who is greatly feared and respected."

"You can eat and drink and work and sleep with a clear conscience?" asked Anthony.

"He stands well with the politicians," Vincent continued. "His name is Al Karley."

"You can go to bed with your wife when you know in your heart you're not a man?"

For a moment, Vincent said nothing. He poured a glass of wine. He drank slowly. He pushed the bottle toward Anthony Boda.

"Sometimes, Tony, you go too far."

"I'm sorry," said Anthony. "I . . . forgive me. No matter how angry I am with a man, I have no right to enter his bedroom."

"I understand," Vincent said. "What I wanted to say was, sometimes you go too far trying to prove you're an American, understand? To be honest with you, Tony, people think you're a crank."

"And what do you think, Vincent?"

"What do I think?" Vincent replied. "What do I think? I think, maybe, you're being . . . too serious about this thing."

"And maybe, Vincent, you're not serious enough."

"Excuse me, Tony," said Vincent. He got up from

the table. An elderly couple had entered the restaurant. Anthony could hear Vincent greet them warmly, seat them at a table, and call to Giulietta, the waitress to serve them. He returned to the table. "You know those people?" he asked Anthony. He didn't wait for a reply. "I don't think you do. Anyhow. Very old, very quiet. Like to eat the best. Anyhow, they're why I have to belong to the Association. Listen, Tony, at first I felt bad to pay these dogs for protection. You're right. I couldn't eat, I couldn't sleep."

"You couldn't come to me for help?" Anthony asked.

"No. And then, one day, I asked myself, why? Why should I feel bad? I paid the government to protect me—but the government failed me. There would be arguments in here. Fights. Respectable people were afraid to come in. What was I supposed to do, call the police? I called the police. But they would always show up after the damage was done. They would walk in here, with the pad and the pencil. 'What was their names?' Did I know their names! 'What did they look like?' They looked like bums, hoodlums, scum of the earth, that was what they looked like! And everything would be written down in a little book. One thing you have to say for the police in America, Tony, they know how to write! Sometimes, I think it's all they do. So, a few nights later, the same thing. The writers come back.

The same questions. The same nothing. So, one day this animal comes in from the Association, I paid him his money."

"But it's wrong!" Anthony insisted. "It's wrong."

"It's another tax, Tony. But this time, I get what I pay for."

"You mean, you will not fight these swine?" asked Anthony.

There was just a hint of impatience in Vincent's voice,

"Tony! What is it? A few dollars? It won't make you. It won't break you."

"I see," said Anthony.

"What do you see?" asked Vincent.

"I will have to fight him alone," answered Anthony. He stood up to go. Vincent picked up the bottle.

"Have another glass of wine, Anthony."

"No, thank you," Anthony replied. And he was surprised and troubled at how formal he sounded. Anthony and Vincent. Born in the same village. Friends from babyhood. Closer than brothers. Married to sisters. How they gloried in their very special relationship. But now, for the first in almost fifty years, they no longer stood together. Each felt the existence of a rift between them. Could it be repaired. Would it grow wider and deeper? They looked at each other, uneasily.

"I have to go," said Anthony.

There was trouble at home, too. Anna-Maria was angry. And Anna-Maria, being no ordinary woman, displayed her anger in no ordinary way. Not for Anna-Maria the loud hysteria or the moody silence. Anna-Maria scorned both vituperation and tears. Anna-Maria struck with courtesy and kindness. Especially at mealtimes.

"This chicken is the best I ever tasted," said Anthony.

"Be happy, Anthony," said Anna-Maria.

"How can I be unhappy?" he asked. "After last night's veal."

"Tomorrow night," said Anna-Maria, "lasagna. I want this to be the best week you ever had."

"Why?" he asked.

"Because," she answered calmly. "It will very likely be the last week of your life."

He put down his knife and fork. "What does that mean?"

"The Association," she answered.

"The Association?" he asked. "What Association?"

"Anthony," she said patiently, "Louis told me all about it."

"Louis!" Anthony shouted angrily. "What right does Louis have to worry his mother about business things! Since when is a woman supposed to be concerned with . . ."

"This is America," she interrupted, "Women in

America do strange, unheard of things. For example, in America, there is the divorce."

"The divorce!" he was taken aback. "Woman, there is such a thing as blasphemy! I know I'm not as strict as I should be when it comes to Church, but . . ."

"That's true." Again, she interrupted. "That's why I must go twice as often to make up for it."

"Then you should know," he said solemnly, "even to say the word is a sin."

She was undaunted. "As an American woman, I have a right to get the divorce."

"Woman," he was about to lose his temper, "What are you saying?"

"Louis is frightened," she said.

"Why? Why is Louis frightened?" he demanded.

"Because you are about to do something stupid," she answered. "Anthony, there is no way in this world here below, that you can defy those thieves."

He nodded, impatiently. "Let me tell you what you have just told me. This is America!"

"Anthony," she said. "The man's name is Al Karley."

"Here in America," Anthony proclaimed, "One is not forced to live in fear of bandits."

"This Al Karley," she continued, "he is what's known as a boss."

"Not my boss."

She placed her hand on his arm. "Anthony, America is a wonderful place. But it is neither a utopia nor a paradise. In some ways, all countries are alike. There is the good and also the bad."

"I want you to listen to me," he said. "I know I could never again look at my face in the mirror, if I bowed down to these mongrel dogs. And those shall be the last words spoken in this house on that subject."

She chose a particularly succulent chicken breast and placed it on his plate. "No, Anthony, the last words spoken on that subject in this house are these: You will pay those people."

He threw his fork down on the table. "Are you telling me how to run my shop." He was visibly disturbed. "I never in my life laid a hand on you in anger! Ha! What way is that to handle a woman so many of my friends ask me! And *your* friends! Don't they say to you—'If he doesn't beat you, isn't it a sign that he doesn't love you?' I want you to remember! Even back in the old country before we came here, I treated you like an American woman! I may have been too good, too liberal. But I warn you. Do not abuse my generosity. Behave like a woman and I will treat you like a woman!"

She waited patiently for him to finish. "You will pay these people, Anthony Boda."

"Anna-Maria, I have given you warning."

"You will pay these people," she said. "We are in America, where a woman is as good as a man. I even vote. And, if I can decide who will be the president in America, I can also have a say in my own home. And I say—you will pay these people."

"And I say never," said Anthony Boda.

Never. But how can a man say "never" to a woman and mean it if he really loves her. And even the gentlest rains erode the hardest rocks. As the week wore on, never became, "All right, I'll think about it!" And then, an angry "maybe," and finally, "All right! All right! I'll pay it, leave me alone!" The surrender was complete. She knew it. She knew the price he was paying in what he considered to be his manhood. She was only trying to save his life, but he could only believe she was letting him down. When he made his decision, she burst into tears. He put his arms around her. Never, even if he lived forever, would he understand this woman.

"What do you want? What do you want now," he demanded. "You got your way. Can't you be happy!"

She kissed him quickly, ran into the bedroom and slammed the door. He looked at the clock above the kitchen stove. It was getting late, and this morning, he wanted to be early at the shop. For a very special reason. He finished his coffee. Then, he walked slowly downstairs to the street corner. This morning, he did something he had never done before. He crossed the street, even though the light was against him. And there was no pause for a prideful glance at the lettering of the shop sign, either. He went inside, removed his coat, hung it on the peg, sat down at his bench and started to cut some leather pieces. Louis looked up from his work.

"Poppa?"

"Yes?" answered Anthony.

"Poppa, I don't think you should be here." There was no missing the embarrassment in the boy's voice.

"Why not?" asked Anthony.

"Because . . ." Louis stopped. Obviously, he was reluctant to say more. Anthony knew why. But, angry himself, he was determined to give no comfort to his son. He pressed the question. "Because?"

"Poppa, he'll be here any minute." Louis said no more. But Anthony decided to rub both their noses in the dirt.

"And you would rather I did not witness the shameful transaction that is soon to take place."

"Poppa," his son was imploring him. "You don't have to be involved with it."

Anthony ran his hand across the leather knife. He picked up a whetstone. He made an elaborate ceremony of sharpening the blade. "You mean, I should pretend the thing does not exist. And if I pretend long enough, hard enough—I will actually believe it and . . . and delude myself into thinking I'm an honorable man."

"Poppa" said Louis. "It's just you got a short fuse.

And with you, one word can lead to another. And you know what I mean."

Anthony tested the knife edge again. "If I must submit, I will submit in silence. Silence."

"You know what they say, Poppa. Silence is golden."

Anthony began to work on his leather again. "Who says that? Cowards?"

And there was silence between them for several long minutes. Finally, it was broken by Louis.

"Poppa, look at it this way, huh? You're a shoemaker, I'm a shoemaker. But I'll get married. I'll have kids. They'll go to school in America. I mean *college*. They won't have to live the way we do."

The knife needed more edge. He picked up the stone again.

"Louis, wine that is sour in the bottom of the bottle is also sour on the top. If the payment of tribute is how one must live in this country—then the rich pay their share as well as the poor."

Louis glances unhappily at his wrist watch. "Go home, Poppa, please."

"No," said Anthony. "I must see this thing with my own eyes. Besides, it's too late. See? The jackal stands in the doorway."

The little silver bell tinkled merrily, even though it was Chuck who entered. With a wave of his hand that took in the entire shop, he said, "Well! Happy

Days! To Anthony Boda and Son, like the sign reads ona window!"

"I will pay the money, Louis," said Anthony.

"But, Poppa . . ."

"I'm closer to the register," said Anthony. He pressed the no sale button. The drawer slid open.

"Well, this is a gloomy-lookin' group," Chuck said. "Whatsamatter? No hello? No how areya! No what's new, how's tricks! Where's all 'at old world courtesy I been hearin' about!"

Anthony removed a five and a ten dollar bill from the register. He held them toward Chuck. "Here's your blood money." Chuck blinked his eyes. "Hey, Louie, what bit your Old Man, huh?"

"Take the money and get out," said Anthony.

The smile had completely vanished from Chuck's face.

"What's eatin' you, Pop?" he demanded.

"I don't like to be called Pop by a common thug."

"Whadya say, Pop?" Chuck's face was impassive now and there was no anger in his tone.

"Please, Poppa," and there was desperation in Louis' voice. He turned to Chuck. "He doesn't mean it."

"Sure, Pop," said Chuck. "You don't mean it, right?"

"I never spoke a single word I didn't mean," said Anthony Boda.

"You got no call talkin' to me like that," said

Chuck. "I'm a guy. I got a job. I work for a livin' like anybody else. So, you better take that back, ya hear? I mean, I'm a person. I'm human. I got feelin's. So, I'm warnin' ya. Ya better take that back. Go ahead."

"He takes it back, he takes it back," exclaimed Louis.

"No. Leave *him* say it. Ya gotta say ya take it back."

"And if I take it back—what will be changed? You will still be the scum of the gutter," said Anthony.

There was a quick movement of Chuck's right hand and the sound of a loud, hard slap as he struck Anthony Boda across the face. The edge of the ring he wore on his little finger had evidently scratched Anthony's nose, and a bright trickle of red blood ran down past Anthony's mouth to his chin. The smile now reappeared on Chuck's face. He shook his hand in the air, ostentatiously, as if to cool it off.

"Louis," he said, "Explain to th' Old Boy what th' score is, huh?"

But before the terrified Louis could speak, Anthony turned to his son. "Louis, explain why you stand by while this animal attacks your father."

The smile on Chuck's face expanded into a laugh. "Hey, Pop! Are you for real! Whadya wan' him to do!"

Anthony shrugged. "Well, he could do this!"

Suddenly the fingers of Anthony Boda's left hand seized Chuck by the throat. His right fist smashed into Chuck's nose. There was a scream of pain and a gush of blood. Caught completely off-guard, Chuck had been too surprised to move but now, he tried to lash out at Anthony, who disregarded his efforts and kept hammering his fist at Chuck's head. Desperately, Chuck started to paw at his back pocket, trying to reach his revolver. Louis, who had been transfixed with fright, finally managed to shout, "Poppa! He's got a gun!"

Anthony seemed to pay no attention—nor did the fusillade of punches subside. At length, the gasping Chuck, mad with pain, managed to get hold of his gun. At that moment, Anthony's left hand released its grip on Chuck's neck and closed over Chuck's wrist. Slowly, he twisted Chuck's gun hand until there was a terrible snapping sound and a horrible scream from Chuck who fainted and fell to the floor. For almost a full minute, Anthony Boda looked down at the bloody heap on the floor. Anthony was breathing hard, as if his lungs were about to burst and, indeed, he was afraid they would. He had been in fights before, but never had he felt such anger. Never had he displayed so much hatred and fury. It had been as if he were striking out at Evil Incarnate, that this miserable wretch represented all injustice and misery—and was personally responsible for all

114

the heartbreaking unfairness in the world. He was frightened by this new awareness of himself, this capacity for violence. And then, he considered how stupid it was. After all, he was still a powerful man, but the bandit was also strong and many years younger. And armed. Therefore, he had bet his life on his own quickness and strength. A foolish thing to do. He also remembered his own father's fate. But what really frightened him was the fact that he had broken his word to Anna-Maria. This fight was what she had foreseen. This was what she had made him promise to prevent. He shook his head sadly. There could be consequences of all kinds; and from many quarters. But, in his heart, he knew that this had been the only course of action he could live with—or die with. So, the battle had begun. For better, for worse, it must now be fought out to the end. And this, after all, was America, not the old country. He became aware of Louis, who was standing absolutely still, too terrified to move. He sighed. The boy was of a different mold. Not worse—not better—just different.

"Louis," he spoke the name gently. "Louis?"

His voice seemed to break a spell. The words poured in anguish from Louis' lips, "Poppa! Poppa! Do you know what you did! Do you know who he is! Poppa! What are we going to do now?"

"Everything will be all right, Louis," said Anthony Boda, reassuringly, "Everything will be all right."

"But what are we going to do, Poppa!"

Anthony Boda reached down to the floor. He grabbed the unconscious Chuck by the hands and swung him up and across his shoulders. "What are we going to do, Louis? Go out. Find a taxi-cab. We will deposit this ... this refuse ... this ... human garbage at the police station."

Lt. Francis Xavier O'Hara, nicknamed Red—although the reason for it had almost completely disappeared from his head—sincerely believed he had seen everything in twenty-eight years as a cop. But this big, barrel-chested foreigner was giving him grounds for second thoughts. Actually, he had no right to call the man a foreigner. After all, who were the Irish to be putting on airs? And the man definitely had some kind of education. He had the accent, but he did speak nicely. And the words! Jeez, the words! When was the last time a citizen had come into the station house with words like those! Words about the duties and obligations of Americans, and so forth and so on. That is, when had somebody ever spoken like that, but *done* something about it, too! He had really worked the hood over, hadn't he? Jeez! Here's a punk who'd never again breathe through his nose the rest of his life! And his whole right arm would always bother him when it rained, too. Chuck Perry. One of Al Karley's goons. Was it possible? Red O'Hara's heart began to pound a little bit quicker. Was it possible that, finally, it could happen? Was this the first breach in what had always been considered as the invincible Karley fortress? Had this Goombah somehow probed for, and found, the vulnerable spot? He looked at Anthony Boda, who stood fearless, but without arrogance. By God! Here was the man who could do it— the very first man who was willing to accept the fight. And then, because, after all, he did have the benefit of twenty-eight years as a cop, he became aware of little warning signals in his brain. He owed this man, this Anthony Boda, something. He cleared his throat.

"Ah, Mr. Boda, you say you—beat this man up—because he tried to shake you down?"

"If that means, he wanted to force me to pay him money, then, yes, Lieutenant," answered Anthony.

"Ah, Mr. Boda, you got any witnesses?" O'Hara asked.

"Witnesses? What do you mean, witnesses?"

"Were there other people in the store who may have seen or heard all this?" asked the Lieutenant.

"Other people," exclaimed Anthony. "Naturally! My son, Louis, here!"

"Besides you and your son—anybody else?"

"No. There were three of us," said Anthony. "Me, my son . . . and that pig!"

117

Lt. Red O'Hara looked closely at Louis Boda. The young fellow was just about scared out of his wits. When you have twenty-eight years experience, you need maybe a fraction of a second, to get the picture. And he knew the only decent thing to do. He rose from his chair. He came around to the front of his desk. He placed a friendly arm around Anthony Boda's shoulder.

"You wanna step this way for just a minute, Mr. Boda?"

He escorted Anthony to the far corner of the room where there was a small bench against the wall. He motioned for Boda to sit, and then he sat down next to him. He reached in his shirt pocket for a package of cigarettes and offered one to Anthony Boda.

"Is it all right if I smoke my pipe?" Anthony asked.

O'Hara nodded. Anthony pushed some tobacco into the bowl of his pipe. O'Hara held a match for him, and then lighted a cigarette. For a while, they puffed away in silence.

"That's nice tobacco," said O'Hara.

"Fellow has it in the candy store on the block," said Anthony. "It's called Paisano. You should try some."

"No. Not me," said O'Hara. "Could never get the hang of a pipe. I mean I like the smell of it and all—but only when the other fellow is smokin' it."

Anthony nodded. "It takes a long time to get used to."

"Mr. Boda," said O'Hara, "Each and every word I'm gonna say to you right now, is off the record. You ever quote me and I'll deny it under oath. You get it?"

Anthony Boda drew on his pipe. "What is there to get, Lieutenant?"

"I'm gonna draw a picture," O'Hara said. "OK. Friday noon, I'm at the desk. You come in draggin' a beat-up hoodlum."

"Ah! Then you admit he's a hoodlum!" said Anthony.

"Oh, yes. He got himself a small rep and a long sheet. But that's *all* I know. So, if you wanna press charges . . ."

Anthony interrupted. "Why do you say *if* I want to press charges, Lieutenant? For what other reason would I deposit this trash here?"

"Here's the picture," said O'Hara. "We only have your word that he came in there to shake you down."

"My word?" asked Anthony. "My word and the word of my son . . . and . . . all the shopkeepers in the neighborhood!"

"Suppose all your neighbors dummy up? It could happen. Say they don't wanna get involved, huh? And then, your son—seein' the way the wind is blowin'—decides, maybe, for your own good—in the long run . . ." O'Hara let it stand there.

"You!" exclaimed Anthony, "An officer of the police! Are you telling me I must submit?"

O'Hara sighed. "No. I'm just tryin' to give an honest man the same break we give a crook. You bring in a crook, you have to inform him of his rights, you see?"

"No," said Anthony. "What does this have to do with me?"

"Well, unfortunately," O'Hara said, "There's absolutely no law says an honest citizen's gotta be warned what he can be in for if he brings a charge against a member of the most powerful mob in the city."

"Will you tell me not to press charges?" Anthony asked.

"Like I said, all I'll do is paint the picture. And then you can decide for yourself what it looks like. Your enemy is Al Karley, not that small-time punk. Al Karley, he's got legit businessmen, politicians, judges all in his hip pocket."

"And policemen, too?"

O'Hara nodded. "Policemen, too."

"In that case," said Anthony. "It's time that pocket was slashed open and all those vermin exposed to the light of day."

Was it possible? Could a grown adult man be so naive? Who was this Boda? Where had he spent his life? O'Hara felt he simply had to make the explanation clearer.

"If you bring charges, Mr. Boda, he'll have the best lawyers money can buy. They'll get you on that stand. They'll make hamburger meat outta you."

"I believe in American justice, Lieutenant."

O'Hara realized now that the man would not be moved. Boda simply refused to understand. The man was pathetic. He was also magnificent. "OK, Mr. Boda," he said. "Do this. You say he's the collection guy for the neighborhood?"

"You don't believe me, Lieutenant?" Anthony asked.

"I believe you," O'Hara answered, "But I'm not your problem. You've got to talk to your friends. The other storekeepers. See if they'll identify him, sign affidavits."

"Oh, they will, they will," Anthony replied.

"Listen, Mr. Boda, I been here before," said O'Hara. "Can you be sure they'll back you?"

"Sure, I'm sure. All it needed was for someone to lead the way. How can they refuse me now?"

And that, O'Hara thought to himself, was that. And yet, why should this decent man suffer the indignities that Karley's expensive lawyers would heap on him in the courtroom? It would be a slaughter because O'Hara knew in his bones that there would be no corroborating evidence. Twenty-eight years had taught him that every storekeeper in the neighborhood would be scared off or bought off. A procession of witnesses would troop to the stand. Each would swear he had never seen Chuck Perry. Each would deny that he was the victim of a shakedown racket. And, as each perjured himself, he would hate himself for what he was being forced to do, and then he would begin to hate Anthony Boda for making him do it. And Anthony Boda would also hate them each in turn for their cowardice and desertion. And thus, friendships that had lasted a lifetime would be broken and destroyed. And Anthony Boda would not only lose his case, but his peace of mind and his place in the community. No. O'Hara couldn't let this happen. At least, not until he had another shot at Boda. Jeez! Why couldn't the man see it! Why couldn't he realize that you just don't push people past their own self-interest. Right or wrong, that's the world. He tried a new tack.

"Look, Mr. Boda, as of right now, you're not necessarily in a jam."

"*I'm* not in a jam?" Anthony asked. "Why would *I* be in a jam?"

"Karley don't want rough stuff or publicity. Not if he can help it. He also don't want collection guys who like to beat up customers. You know what I think? He'll yank Chuck outta there and bury him someplace *if* you forget the whole thing."

"Mr. Karley, himself, he told you this?" Anthony asked.

"No, Mr. Boda," answered O'Hara. "But I'm talkin' to you outta twenty-eight years of experience,

122

hard experience. I don't want you to get hurt. And in a lotta ways you just don't realize. Press a charge and I gotta let this hood make a phone call. In fifteen minutes, you're gonna have a lawyer down here. A very expensive lawyer."

Anthony Boda stood up. "You're a man with a good heart, Lieutenant. But it's important for me to discover something."

"Discover what?" O'Hara asked.

"If I did the right thing when I came to America," replied Anthony Boda.

The newspapers seemed to think so, and so did the news broadcasts. He was hailed for his courage. Praised for his sense of duty. He was interviewed and photographed. A well-known clergyman found a text for a sermon in Anthony Boda's action. "For the whole duty of a man is to obey the Commandments. . . ." Everyone smiled at him on the streets. Neighbors patted his back. There was talk that President Roosevelt, himself, was going to send Anthony Boda a personal letter of praise—even invite him to the White House. But that was, of course, a completely groundless rumor. On the other hand, who could really tell? About anything? Anna-Maria said nothing. This was because she understood that there was really nothing to say. Regardless of what was wrong or right—sensible or foolish—it was a time for silence.

Lt. O'Hara came by a few days later.

"Good morning, Mr. Boda."

"Ah, the police lieutenant," said Anthony.

"You'll notice a uniformed man near the store. There's also an extra one around your house. We're gonna protect you every way we can."

"Thank you, Lieutenant."

"No," said O'Hara. "Maybe we oughtta thank you. You're doin' somethin' nobody else has ever had the guts to try. And the papers have caught a hold of it. I see you got 'em all. 'Shoemaker Defies Mob!' 'Shoemaker to Destroy Shakedown Racket!' 'Beginning of the End for Organized Crime?' "

Anthony said, "The papers think we have already won."

"Yeah," said O'Hara, "But it's no good unless you win in court."

"But why are the papers so sure?" Anthony asked.

"Well, Mr. Boda, for the papers, you're today's sensation. Tomorrow, it'll be somebody else."

"What do we need," Anthony wondered, "To be sure of winning?"

"It would be better if we had more witnesses," said O'Hara. "But who knows? Maybe they'll start comin' around? Look. We wanna keep an eye on you, so don't go anyplace without tellin' us."

"Where would I go, Lieutenant?"

When Lt. O'Hara left, Anthony walked down the block to Vincent's Restaurant. Vincent was sitting at a table chatting with some customers. When he saw Anthony, he excused himself immediately. They sat at the far end of the bar. It was quiet and, more or less, private. Vincent poured them each a glass of wine. For a while they drank in silence. When they finished, Anthony said, "Now, Vincent, let me buy you a glass." Vincent nodded and poured again.

"Were the police in here to see you?" asked Anthony.

"Yes," Vincent answered. "Also from the District Attorney."

"So?"

"And he spoke to me, Tony."

"So?"

"Tony." There was a tone of supplication in Vincent's voice. "What do you want from me?"

"Where do you stand, Vincent?" Tony looked straight into Vincent's eyes. Vincent averted his gaze.

"I received another visitor," Vincent said.

"Who?"

"Somebody. He explained certain facts."

"What kind of facts," asked Anthony.

Vincent waved and smiled at a departing customer.

"He explained, this gentleman, that, in order to run my business here, I need a license."

"But you always knew that," said Anthony.

"Yes. I always knew that, Tony." Vincent

nodded his head for emphasis. "But he explained, this gentleman, that when I try to renew my license, there might be . . . problems."

"But you get your license from the government!" Anthony exclaimed, "Not from these hoodlums!"

Vincent nodded again. "Ah, Tony. But you see. This gentleman *is* from the government. That part of the government which sees to these things."

Anthony shook his head. "I don't believe it."

"You don't want to believe it," Vincent said. "Tony! This is not *our* fight! One part of the government says it wants to put Al Karley in jail. Another part says it will support him!"

"I spoke with the lawyers in the District Attorney's Office," Anthony said. "I believe them to be honorable men. They said they will protect me. They will protect you, too."

Once again, Vincent filled their glasses. "I'll think about it," he said.

"What is there to think about?" asked Anthony.

Vincent sighed. "Tony, these things are not so simple."

Anthony set his glass down on the counter. "I see," he said. "You have already thought about it. And you have decided."

For the second time in succession, things between them had ended badly. And this time, on a worse note than before. Anthony walked back to the shop.

He told Louis to go home. Louis protested there was too much work to be finished. But Anthony wanted to be alone. Reluctantly, Louis let him have his way. Anthony picked up his knife. He began to shape a sole. It was remarkable how clearly he could think while he was engrossed in his work. What was he doing? Where was he headed? Obviously, everyone thought he was a fool. True, he was right and they were wrong. But what did it prove? For all that he sang the praises of America, the fact was, Anna-Maria had spoken the truth. In some ways, all countries are alike. The rich and the poor are everywhere. So are the powerful and the weak. Money talks as loudly here as anywhere else. The difference? In America, nobody's birth need condemn him and his children to a lifetime of frustration and poverty. Here, any man might aspire to a position of influence and power. *That* was the difference. He measured the sole carefully. The fact is, he was becoming a character. Even those who respected his courage, considered him a fool. The Irish police lieutenant admired his courage, perhaps, but thought him a fool for rocking the boat. Anna-Maria loved him but, in her heart, she believed him to be a fool. His son Louis was probably ashamed of himself for thinking his father a fool, but that didn't change the fact. Who and what is a fool? A fool is one who is opposed to everyone else. For whatever reason. His own father had been a fool. He felt a chill pass along his spine. It was the very first time he had ever thought of that sainted man in those terms. But what else could he say about Poppa? And wasn't he trying to be the man Poppa was? Perhaps. Yet, Poppa was a fool. Perhaps, it takes more courage to submit than to lash out. Maybe the true strength is the one that enables us to endure. What did Poppa gain by his defiance? A bullet-riddled body. A grieving widow and a fatherless, young son. And his act had neither changed nor settled anything. Bandits and government continued to thrive and prosper in an unholy alliance that only grew stronger. If it hadn't been for the generosity of Vincent's father, widow and child would have starved to death. Vincent. What was he doing to Vincent? For years, Vincent had struggled and saved his money running a lunch counter. Now, he had been able to open a "restaurant". It was the dream of a lifetime come true. Vincent was simply in no position to fight anybody. Funny. A week ago, had any man predicted that the friendship between Anthony and Vincent could come to an end, he would have been dismissed as a lunatic. Well, the friendship was probably foundering right now. It was growing darker. He reached for the light switch and, through the window, he caught sight of the long, black limousine that had just pulled up to the curb. A man, who looked very much like the hoodlum, Chuck, got out. He was the type that wore bandit written all over his face. For a moment, Anthony's fingers tightened on the handle of the knife. At the corner, he could see the special policeman. Surely, the hoodlums were not going to try anything here. Now. Although, who could tell? The bandit opened the rear door of the limousine and an older man emerged. This one was well-built, well-dressed, with a sun-burnt face. He was hatless—the mark of a barbarian—and his grey hair was carefully brushed. His black shoes shone like highly polished mirrors—a sure sign that a man is concerned with his appearance. He walked toward the door. The young bandit started to follow him, but, at a gesture from the older man, he shrugged and returned to the car. The bell tinkled cheerily as the door opened and then closed behind the visitor. As Anthony suspected, there was the smell of a recent visit to a good barbershop about the man. He approached the counter and stood there silently. Anthony took another stitch in the sole of the shoe and then slowly set down the work. He rose to his feet and looked at the stranger.

"I see you sew by hand," the man said. "You sew good, too. I oughtta know. My father was a shoemaker. You Anthony Boda?"

Anthony nodded, "What can I do for you?"

"That depends," the man answered.

"On what?" Anthony asked.

"On you. I can be your best friend or your worst enemy."

129

"And what is your business here?" Anthony asked.

"My name is Karley," the visitor answered. "Al Karley. You heard of me."

"I heard," Anthony said. "I cannot say I like what I heard."

"But I like what I heard about you," Al Karley said. "They tell me you're a man."

"So?"

"So," Al Karley said, "You shouldn't be concerned with that ... with that ... little situation ... that happened here a few days ago."

"Why not?" asked Anthony.

"Because it's beneath you," Karley snapped.

"I will not be slapped by hoodlums," said Anthony.

"Of course, not," Karley agreed. "But it's more blessed to give than to receive, if I might quote the Scripture."

"How dare you quote the Holy Book?" Anthony's voice was edged with contempt.

Karley's answer was matter-of-fact. "My name is Al Karley. I dare anything. What's the problem here? You gave better than you got. So? Forget it."

Anthony shook his head. "This matter is now in the hands of the law."

Karley nodded. "Of course. But in whose hands is the law? In the hands of the man who can buy better lawyers, better witnesses, better juries, better judges."

"Why do you tell me all this?" asked Anthony.

Karley smiled. "I like you."

For a moment, Anthony was incredulous. "You like me?"

Karley raised his palms. "I'm a man of great wealth. I can afford to like all sorts of people."

"What do you want?" asked Anthony Boda.

"This case," replied Karley, "Against my . . . my . . ." he groped for a word. He couldn't come up with it. He shrugged. "Well, he *is* scum, isn't he? That's neither here nor there. What I'm saying is, his case must not come to trial."

"Why not?" asked Anthony.

"I have read the Bible," Karley answered.

"Really?" Anthony seemed amused by the idea. "A pity you didn't take it more seriously."

"Mind if I sit down?" Karley asked. Without waiting for an answer, he pulled a small wire-backed chair close to the counter and sat. He removed what appeared to be a solid gold cigarette case from his breast pocket. He opened it and held it toward Anthony who disregarded his offer. Karley then selected a cigarette. He replaced the case and then brought a shining silver lighter from his coat pocket. He lighted the cigarette, inhaled deeply, removed it from his mouth, and regarded the glowing tip. "Way back," he said, "Oh a coupla thousand years ago at least, a certain match was arranged. You musta read about it. The fight between David and Goliath. Now, who woulda bet on David? Nobody

131

with brains. Do I have to tell you the smart money took a bath?"

"In other words," Anthony said, "You're afraid you can be beaten."

Karley shrugged. "The chance? One in a million. Still, why risk it? The take from all you store-keepers—nickles and dimes. But you add it up. It's a good dollar. It takes care of the overhead. Keeps the labor force busy. You see what I mean?" He didn't wait for a comment. He continued.

"I'm after other stuff. Much bigger. A lot better. Drop the charges."

Anthony shook his head.

Karley filled his lungs with smoke and exhaled very slowly. "Tell you something, Tony. I'm break-ing away, gradually, from all this rough stuff. I got a daughter. She goes to college. American society girls go to that college. We have to be respectable. We got an image to consider."

"This daughter of yours," said Anthony, "She knows, of course, what her father does? Really does?"

There was no answer from Karley. He dropped the cigarette on the floor, ground it out and lit another.

"Ah," nodded Anthony. "I see."

"Anthony," said Karley suddenly, "Get out of here. Come with me!"

"Do you want to take me for a ride," asked Anthony.

"Yeah. Yeah, I guess you could say that," replied Karley. "I need a guy like you."

"To do what?" asked Anthony.

"To help me run my organization," Karley answered.

Despite himself, Anthony smiled. "No. You don't want me."

Karley had an interesting manner of smoking. It gave away what he was thinking. When he had something important in mind, he held the butt between his forefinger and thumb and puffed away steadily. "Don't you tell me what I want. I'll tell you what I have to get. Plenty of guys got guts. Plenty of guys got brains. But you're one of the very few guys that got both. What are you killin' yourself in a shoestore, huh?"

"I'm a shoemaker by profession," said Anthony.

Karley needed a fresh cigarette. "Nobody's a shoemaker by profession! Come on!"

"I didn't come to this country to be a bandit."

"Let me tell you why you came to this country," Al Karley said, starting the cigarette. "You came to this country for the same reason I did. You thought the streets were paved with gold."

Anthony considered for a moment. "Yes, that was part of the reason."

"Well, my side of the street is shiny bright. Cross over, Tony!"

"You don't want me, Karley," Anthony said.

What was there about Karley that reminded him of another bandit, a long time ago. A man on a huge, black horse who rode across the field and paused at the door of the farmhouse. It was the grin. The expression of contempt for all who were beneath him; the grin which so plainly said: "You, all of you, are dirt who live and die at my pleasure." Once again, he could see his father's face. He could see the vein along his father's temple begin to throb—just as he could now feel the blood starting to pound inside his own. He wanted to seize this immaculately groomed animal by the throat and choke the life out of him, but he knew he would prove nothing, just as his father's act had proved nothing. He took a deep breath to compose himself.

"Let me tell you why you don't want me," he said, finally. "If I ever decide to become what you are now, there would not be room for both of us in the same organization."

Karley laughed. "You'd be surprised, Anthony, at how much room there is in this world. And how much money."

"I don't think you understand me, Karley."

"And I don't think you understand me, Boda. I came here why? Because I want to avoid bloodshed."

"Is that a fact?" Anthony asked. "And since when does a wolf shy away from blood?"

"I warn you, Anthony Boda!"

"Mr. Karley," said Anthony Boda. "You wear an expensive suit, like a gentleman. You try to talk like a gentleman. But nothing helps. You fool no one. You're still a hoodlum."

Karley rose to his feet. "And you're still a chump. You'll never know what hit you." He walked out of the shop.

Anthony watched the young bandit open the door of the car. Karley got in, and soon the car roared away from the curb.

Anthony returned to his leather. Every man's fate is ordained. It may not be the fate he likes or might select for himself, if given a choice—but it was the fate he would have to live with—and die with. Anthony Boda was fated to be a fool. There was no use fighting it and no point in trying to change it. It was fate. It was also six o'clock. Time to close the shop. Time to go home to dinner, or was it supper? Whatever it was, it was certainly time to dispel the moody silence that had been hanging over the Boda household. Time they went back to the singing and joking and everything else that had made their lives together a pleasure. As he put on his coat, he began to whistle.

That night, turned out, indeed, to be a happy one at the modest flat of Anthony Boda. It was quite another story the following morning in the luxurious penthouse of Al Karley. The interview with Anthony Boda was not the only thing that had gone wrong. The approaching case was getting under his skin. Why it should be bothering him so much was hard to say. He just had a hunch, that's all—and he was a man who lived by hunches. That was because a psychiatrist had explained to him that what we call hunches are, in truth, sudden insights which are based on the accumulation of stored subconscious knowledge and experience. Or, something like that. Everything about the Boda situation was bad. He didn't like the way the case was making the papers. Plus the insinuations that he, Al Karley, was the villain behind it all. David and Goliath. And once the public sees it that way, David can't lose. And the judge who had been assigned to the trial. Dammit, why hadn't a reliable judge been chosen! Who fell asleep on that one? For a judge, they picked a paisan—the son of an immigrant—who would bend over backwards to prove that just because a man's name ended in a vowel, it didn't mean that he and the vast majority of his fellow-countrymen supported Organized Crime. This was a case that cried for a WASP! A nice, dignified, reliable WASP who would dismiss the charges, as they deserved to be dismissed, and everyone would say it was on the basis of evidence. The paisan would see himself as a man with a mission— and maybe he was. There was a rumor the FBI was nosing around. Every couple of years, somebody high in the rackets was made an example of and hustled off to jail just to keep the public happy. Was this to be *his* year? Well, this case must not come to trial. He would have to stop it, somehow.

In the midst of these heavy deliberations, he heard a voice, a voice he cherished above all else in this world or the next.

"Hello, Daddy."

He looked up. She was standing in front of him. He jumped to his feet. He hugged her and kissed her.

"Marissa! Marissa, Honey! Let me look at you!"

She had long, blonde hair, deep blue eyes, one of those cute, turned up noses. She looked just like some classy Protestant debutante. He couldn't believe she was his own flesh and blood. He never stopped marveling at the thought.

"Marissa, shouldn't you be in school?"

She nodded. "Yes, Daddy," she replied.

Something in the tone, something strange, something frightening. His every sense was alerted.

"Something wrong?" he asked apprehensively. Now, he could see her eyes were troubled. And it wasn't little girl trouble, either about a dress or a doll. She was old enough for trouble with a guy. A surge of anger swept through him. If some young punk had even ... He forced himself to be calm, very calm. He even managed a smile.

"Do you have a cigarette, Daddy?" she asked.

It annoyed him that she smoked. But she was old enough and what could you do? He held a light for her. He noticed, with satisfaction, that she was an awkward smoker. She probably did it for effect rather than make a habit of it. Actually, after a few shallow drags, she stubbed out the butt in an ashtray. She looked at him and the trouble in her eyes seemed more pronounced than ever.

"There are stories in the paper," Marissa said. "And all my friends read them. And they said to me, 'Of course, it isn't *your* Dad!' And I said, 'Of course, not! It's another Al Karley.' And ... ah ... the reason ... the reason I came down here ..."

"... was to ask me." He finished it for her.

She was very close to tears. "Daddy, I didn't know what to think!"

He placed his hands on her shoulders. He looked into her eyes and smiled. "It *is* another Al Karley, Baby."

She threw her arms around him, joyously. "I knew it! I knew! Daddy can you ever forgive me!"

"Forget it, Baby! Tell me. Have you met some nice guy?"

She smiled. "Oh. No one special. You'll have to be my best boy-friend for a while yet."

"Listen," he said. "You hungry? Let's get something to eat."

She shook her head. "I'm watching my weight and you don't need it. Let's just sit and chat for a bit. Then I have to go back to school."

"How's school?" he asked.

"Daddy, it's just fantastic!" Her eyes lit up. "Next weekend, I've been invited to go home with Enid Schofield! That's *the* Schofields!"

"Hey! That's all right!"

"She has a cousin and he happened to see my picture! No! I better not say anymore! He's a senior at Yale and ... no! I don't want to hex this! He's Phi Beta but he also happens to be captain of the water polo team! Daddy, that's the toughest sport there is! So, he's the perfect combination of brains and ... no! I've said too much already! We'll just have to wait and see what happens!"

Did it matter what she was saying? No. Just to hear her talk! Just to hear that beautiful music in her voice. To see that beautiful smile dancing on her lips, it was enough to make a man's heart break with joy!

"Daddy! Are you listening?"

Of course, he was listening. What was she saying now?

She reached up and smoothed a lock of his hair, "Daddy, would you mind terribly if I changed my major? I've decided *finally*! I want sociology!"

"Ah, you go right ahead, Baby! You do whatever you want," he said, happily.

"I want to work with the poor children. Some of us have decided to rent a store or something—in the colored section—and help the children study the core subjects."

"Umhm," he said. "And where you gonna get the money?"

She smiled at him. "We thought we'd . . . raise it . . . somehow."

He snapped his fingers. "What do you know! You just raised it!"

She kissed him, "Daddy, you are an *angel*!"

"I'll pay the rent and buy the books. And you tell me what else you need!"

"Daddy, we'll call it the Karley Learning Center after our wonderful benefactor."

He shook his head. "No, Baby. You gotta keep me out of it, understand?"

"Oh, Daddy, sometimes, I wish you weren't so . . . modest!"

"It's my nature, Honey. Remind me to give you a check."

"Oh, Daddy!" she held him very tightly. "You're so generous."

He laughed. "I'm getting off cheap. I was afraid you'd ask for the moon. And I'd have to reach up and grab it, somehow."

"For a moment, her smile disappeared. And a trace of the troubled look returned to her eyes.

"About . . . the other thing, Daddy . . . How could I have even thought . . . what got into me, anyhow!"

"Forget it," he smiled. "A bad dream."

"No." She nestled against him. "What I did was

forget what it says in the Bible you bought me. 'Honor Thy Father.' "

This little girl, oh, this little girl! Well, maybe she wasn't a little girl, anymore. Back in the old country, she'd be married and with kids by this time—just like her momma had been. Ah, but Marissa would never be a momma, fat, dumpy, worn out with childbirth and drudgery. Marissa would be a mother. A society pages matron. An exquisitely gowned hostess to the top people in America. Why not? She was part of that crowd right now. Why couldn't she marry into it? He would buy her way in or blast her way in, but in she would go, one way or another. And her children, they would be raised by nurses and governesses, maids and butlers. What was he killing himself for? Why was he moving heaven and earth? For whom? For her! All the dough that was being ground out of horseplayers, whores, and storekeepers. Every loan-shark dollar that was chewed from the flesh of thousands of victims. Every nickel of tribute checked off the wages of terrified dressmakers and profane truckdrivers, all of it was being cleaned and converted into legit operations. All of it would be in her name. She would own banks, real estate, department stores, restaurants, factories. She'd be able to buy and sell; wheel and deal with the biggest and best of them. Turn her down? How could Society turn her down? The Schofields? He had read all about great-grandfather Schofield. Here was a bandit who slaughtered hundreds of Indians, shot down scores of strikers, swindled thousands of widows, owned entire state legislatures, bought senators, congressmen, mayors, and judges in wholesale batches, and even had one president of the U. S. on his hip! And the *Schofields* would object to Marissa? He sighed happily.

"What are you thinking of, Daddy?" she asked.

"Oh," he answered lazily, "I'm thinking it's time you went back to school, that is, if you're going."

He was also thinking something else, which, of course, he had no intention of ever telling her. He had the nagging idea that Anthony Boda could somehow transform this beautiful dream he had for her into a nightmare. Therefore, Anthony Boda had to be hit and the sooner the safer.

Louis Boda was busy sewing on a full sole. He felt his father tap him on the shoulder. Louis reached for the switch and shut down the machine.

"See what it says here in the newspaper, Louis?" Anthony displayed the sheet proudly. The headline ran halfway across the page. "Boda Sticks to His Guns!" Louis leaned forward to read the item. "Anthony Boda sticks to his guns or, rather, defies the guns of the mob. Here, finally, is an American citizen who has decided he's had enough. He will not submit to extortion. 'I will not be intimidated,' said Anthony Boda. 'I don't care what it costs me! Mil-

142

lions for defense—but not one cent for tribute!' "
Louis looked up from the paper. "Did you say *that*,
Poppa?"

Anthony laughed. "No, I didn't say that, but the
reporters, they like to put the words in your mouth."

Louis sighed. No. Poppa didn't say that exactly—
but he could have. That kind of statement described
Poppa to a "T." It's what Poppa had meant and
what Poppa had felt. "Poppa," he said, "I wish I
were like you."

"But you are like me," Anthony protested. "You're
my own son!"

"No, Poppa," Louis shook his head. "Very few
people are just like you. You were born at the wrong
time. You should have lived when there were great
heroes and kings and fighters."

"My son," said Anthony, "We always need
fighters."

"I know I failed you, Poppa. I stood there and
did nothing while ... while ..." He was overcome
with shame. His eyes filled with tears. He could say
no more. The store was silent except for his sobbing.

Anthony felt sorrow and a sudden flash of anger—at
himself. What had he done to his boy? Louis was
just like his mother. Violence of any kind was alien
to him. Anna-Maria and Louis. Both relied on charm
and laughter. But lately, Louis was laughing no longer. Why couldn't Louis be let alone? And like his
mother, he would prevail in other ways. Perhaps,

better ways. Sometimes, the fate of a fool ordains that he become a crusader chief. It can be a lonely life for a man. It's no bed of roses for his wife and children, either.

"I'm frightened, Poppa," said Louis.

"There's nothing to be afraid of Louis," said Anthony. "Nothing."

"Yes, Poppa," said Louis. But, of course, he didn't believe it.

Louis went back to work. Anthony watched him. How quick. How skillful. A crazy thought crossed his mind. What if, somehow, he could have a miracle. What if, in some mysterious way, the time could be turned back. What if, once again, that animal, Chuck, were standing in front of the counter and Anthony had the five and the ten dollar bills ready to hand over. Would he be able to say this time, "Here's your money" instead of "Here's your *blood* money." That's all that would have been necessary. That one word, blood, it had been enough to transform him into a crusader chief and change the world for everybody. If, somehow, that miracle would come to pass, would he leave out the blood? Honestly? He couldn't say. And, now, he was really angry with himself. He was a *complete* fool! And then, he smiled, ruefully. How could he fight it? Wasn't it his fate? He looked up at the door because there was the merry tinkle of the bell.

Anna-Maria entered. She was holding a package.

144

"The mailman brought this upstairs," she said. "It says from the leather company."

"Why would the leather company send a package to the house?" asked Louis.

"Because," Anthony answered, "Christmas is coming! See, how it's addressed? To the Boda Family."

"What could it be?" asked Anna-Maria.

"A calendar," Louis ventured.

"Maybe perfume," said Anna-Maria. "Perfume for me, and cologne for you!"

Suddenly, the shop buzzed and crackled with delighted speculation!

"A radio!" said Louis.

"A toaster!" said Anna-Maria.

"A Bible," said Louis.

"A clock," said Anthony.

"Wait!" shouted Louis. "A clock! That's right, Poppa!" He held the package to his ear. "I can hear it ticking!"

"Hear what ticking?" asked Anthony. "Let me!"

He took the package and placed it close to his head.

"I don't hear anything. You sure?"

"It must be my imagination, Poppa."

Anthony smiled at his son. "That's your trouble, Louis, you live too much in your imagination."

"And what's wrong with imagination?" demanded Anna-Maria, rising instantly to the defense of her son. "On my side of the family, people had great visions. My folk were preachers and poets."

"Well, it's time to get back to work," said Anthony. "On my side of the family, people always earned a living."

"Shouldn't we open the package, Anthony," Anna-Maria asked.

"It's addressed to the home. Let's open it in the home. Tonight. After supper."

"How can you live like this!" exclaimed Anna-Maria. "Have you no curiosity? How can you wait another minute!"

Anthony threw his hands in the air. "All right. Louis, open the package."

Eagerly, Louis' fingers tore at the paper wrapping. As the first piece was ripped away, there was a sudden, sharp popping noise. Instantly, Anthony Boda knew! He *knew*! The word for bomb flashed in his brain. But before that word could be transformed into a warning shout from his lips—there was a searing, blinding flash of light and a deafening, earth-shaking blast. But none of them ever heard the sound.

Lt. Francis Xavier (Red) O'Hara stopped at the nurses' station on the surgical floor. "How is Mr. Boda?" he asked.

The grey-haired nurse looked up from a chart. "The same, I guess. He'll live. Not that he seems to give a damn."

146

"Doctor say anything today?" asked O'Hara.

The nurse shrugged. O'Hara walked down the corridor. A uniformed man was standing guard at the door. They acknowledged each other with nods. O'Hara looked at the burly patrolman, laden with heavy equipment—revolver, handcuffs, sap, club, the works. It was the old story—horses and barn doors. He approached the bed. Boda was lying very still. Tonight, his eyes were open. He was staring at the ceiling.

"Mr. Boda," said O'Hara, quietly. "It's me, Lt. O'Hara. I didn't know if you were asleep. I wasn't gonna wake you." He paused but Boda remained motionless.

"They say you could be outta here in a while," O'Hara continued. "Ah ... I ... we ... all of us are very sorry. I know nothing can bring back your wife and your son." He stopped. There was simply nothing more to be said. He didn't know whether to go or to stay. And then, Anthony Boda turned his head toward him. He looked up into O'Hara's eyes.

"Tell me, Lieutenant," he said quietly. "Anna-Maria, Louis. Why were they killed at once, while I received only scratches?"

"I don't know," O'Hara answered. "Fellows at the Bomb Squad were talkin' about it. It's a technical thing. It has to do with the ... ah ... angle of forces and stuff like that."

"No," said Anthony. "I mean what reason? Why

147

had God seen fit to spare me and take, instead, my wife and son, both of whom were finer human beings than I can ever hope to be?"

"For that answer, you'd have to ask a priest."

"I have asked a priest," said Anthony Boda. "And he said that ... God's ways follow mysterious designs. So you see, I'm no wiser than before."

"I'm sorry about the trial," O'Hara said. "That is, I'm sorry we didn't have one."

"It doesn't matter," said Anthony Boda.

"Chuck Perry, the hood, just disappeared. So, there was no defendant. Karley probably had him hit. He's deep under cement somewhere."

"It doesn't matter, Lieutenant."

"You set an example, Mr. Boda. You woke up a lot of people. They're really after Karley now. Not just us—but the Federals, too."

"It doesn't matter."

"You can't keep saying it doesn't matter, Mr. Boda."

"I think I have finally unraveled the riddle." Anthony Boda nodded his head slightly and closed his eyes for a moment. The thoughts were forming so clearly in his mind now. "You see, Lieutenant, I had become arrogant. And so, I had forgotten the law of nature. The Strong Destroy the Weak. I had seen my pictures in the newspapers. And my head was turned. I forgot who I was: an immigrant shoemaker, a nothing, a nobody. I behaved as if I were

148

an owner, an owner of lawyers, judges, politicians. I was drunk, not with wine, but with power. Therefore, I didn't listen to men of experience and true wisdom. Men like my friend Vincent. 'It's just another tax! Pay it!' Well, I refused to pay it one way; I was forced to pay it another."

"You can't talk that way, Mr. Boda," said O'Hara.

"But I learned it from you, Lieutenant. Or, I should have learned from you. You were willing to teach me. You remember. What did a great man once write? Discretion is the better part of valor."

"Believe me, Mr. Boda," said O'Hara. "We'll bust up that mob. Karley figures maybe he can ride out this particular storm the way he survived some others. But he won't."

"That's true. Because I will kill him," said Anthony Boda.

"You can't make your own justice, Mr. Boda." said Lt. O'Hara.

"I think I'll sleep now," said Anthony. He closed his eyes. The lieutenant was a fine man. But he was beginning to become a bother. What did he mean, you can't make your own justice? Isn't that, very often, the only kind of justice there is? But there was little point in the conversation. Indeed, the time for all conversation had ended. There was but one thing that mattered now—the death of Al Karley. And the death of Al Karley could have meaning only if it came at the hands of Anthony Boda. He must kill

Karley himself. Not even the law itself, had the right to cheat him of his revenge. He opened his eyes. Lt. O'Hara was gone. The room was dark. But Anthony Boda was in an even greater darkness. The bright beacon light that had once been America, had flickered finally, and died.

He walked into Vincent's Restaurant. Vincent was at his table in the back, paying his bills. Anthony sat down opposite. He poured himself a glass of wine and another one for Vincent.

"Hello," he said.

Vincent raised his glass. "I didn't think you'd ever speak to me again, Tony."

"We've been friends too long, Vincent."

Vincent sighed. "Yes. I forgot that. I should have agreed to be a witness. Not because it was right or wrong. But because a friend asked me. I spoke to your lieutenant. I said to him you can count on us. And he can rely on every man in this neighborhood. Those who refuse will have to settle accounts with me."

"But none of that will bring back Anna-Maria and Louis," said Anthony quietly. "They must be avenged."

Vincent stared at him. "What are you saying, Tony?"

"I must kill this animal, this Al Karley," said Anthony without heat or emotion of any kind. "I must kill him personally."

Vincent shook his head vigorously. "Tony, this kind of thing—it's not done in America."

For the first time, there was a trace of anger in Anthony's voice. "I am sick and tired of being told what is and what is not done in America. I come to you as a friend. Will you help me?"

"Well," said Vincent. And he paused as if trying to find the words.

"The answer," said Anthony, "is yes—or the answer is no. The answer is not well."

Without a moment's further hesitation, Vincent said,

"The answer is yes." He reached for and clasped Anthony's hand. Then each raised a glass in recognition of the fully repaired friendship.

"The hunting rifle," Anthony said, "the one your father made? There is no better and accurate weapon in the world. It gives me two barrels, the over and the under. I need only two shots. One for Mr. Karley. The other for his bodyguard."

"Oh, no!" said Vincent. "You can't walk around the streets with a rifle!"

"I have studied the habits of this animal. On a Friday night, he slips away from the city. He travels north to visit his college daughter. He rides alone in the car except for the driver who is also the bodyguard. There is a place he must pass where the highway is being mended. He must slow down. That's where I will wait in ambush."

"Can I talk you out of this, Tony?" asked Vincent.

"No."

"Well, when do we go?"

"We?"

"What is a friend, Tony," asked Vincent. "Isn't a friend another gun to stand beside you?"

The superhighway north was being repaired, just as Anthony had stated. The two lanes narrowed into one. There was some fifty feet where the pavement had been broken and the cars had to be driven carefully and, practically at a crawl, over depressions, dirt and rocks. On either side of the lane, were a series of wooden barricades and, one of these formed a perfect hiding place for Anthony and Vincent. They had come here, just north of the city, in Vincent's car. They had hidden the automobile off the road and behind some trees. It was now completely dark. There was nothing to do but wait.

"How do we know he's coming tonight?" asked Vincent.

"If not tonight—then next Friday night," said Anthony.

"How do we know he hasn't been by here already?" Vincent wanted to know.

"You're as nervous as an old lady, Vincent."

"I brought us something to drink, Tony."

"Nothing for me," said Anthony Boda. "Nothing for me until I kill him."

Quietly, Anthony kept cocking and uncocking the hammer of the rifle. It was a beautiful weapon, designed by a master craftsman. Delicately balanced as a watch: the scrollwork on the barrel, the silver inlay of the stock were worthy to be called a work of art. He still remembered the shock he had experienced as a boy when Vincent's father had casually aimed at a passing rabbit and killed the animal in its tracks. It was by no means his first encounter with death. But usually the killing was done with heavy, ugly weapons: misshapen blunderbusses, awkward shotguns, unwieldy pistols. Somehow, he could not consider this lovely, graceful rifle a weapon. It was as if a statue or a painting had suddenly become an instrument of murder. He often wondered about the relationship between art and death. Of course, he couldn't wonder at too great length. He was busy learning the shoemaker's trade. But when he came to America, he was able to read books and listen to the free lectures at the settlement house. Of course, he couldn't understand everything and, at first, he felt bad. Later, he sensed that even those who claimed to know, were just as much in the dark as he was. The thing, evidently, like religion, was at heart shrouded in mystery. The night was cold. But he would be wearing gloves in any event. He knew the moisture

153

in his hands could cause tiny rust spots on the barrel. He regretted the fact that it had been necessary for him to deface the rifle by putting blacking on the barrel so it would not shine in the moonlight. But this disfigurement was only temporary. Tomorrow morning, it would gleam like new. The rush hour was long past. Traffic was almost nonexistent. Three or four minutes could go by without the sight of a single car. Now, one could be heard in the distance. At first, the high whine of a speeding engine. Then a growl, as the driver, warned by the signs, quickly throttled down. Now, the labor of the motor, as the driver slowly picked a path along the rough and rutted roadway. He heard the whispered question from Vincent.

"Tony?"

"Yes." This time, he cocked the piece and kept the hammer back for action. He rested the barrel along the top edge of the barricade. He waited for the car to come abreast. He heard a click. Vincent had released the safety catch of a heavy revolver.

"He belongs to me, Vincent," Anthony said.

"I have a score to settle with him, also," said Vincent.

"Not as great as mine." Anthony sighted carefully.

"That's why you may have the first two shots," said Vincent. "And after that . . ."

"Quiet," said Anthony. "Let me make sure of him."

"Is it the car, Tony?"

"Yes," whispered Tony. "The long, black car."

"Be sure," said Vincent. "There are many long, black cars."

"Oh, yes." There was triumph in Tony's voice. "I can make him out in the moonlight. I can see his depraved, evil face."

"Let him come a little bit closer, Tony," advised Vincent. "Just a little bit closer."

Al Karley was leaning back against the seat. His head was perfectly still. His mouth was open. He was obviously asleep. And that's how he would die. The line from the age-old prayer formed in Anthony's mind. "If I should die before I wake ..." Had Karley said any prayers recently? It didn't matter. Anthony Boda peered through the slit of the rear sight. He found the top of the front sight. He lined it up against Al Karley's temple as the slow moving, laboring limousine came directly abreast. Perfect. He drew a slow, deep breath. He held it. Now, very gently, he squeezed the trigger. The explosion caught him by surprise. But, as the rifle steadied from the recoil, it was still on target. He found the chauffeur's forehead and fired again. The car lurched forward.

"You missed him, Tony!" Vincent shouted, "You missed him!"

The roar of Vincent's revolver close to his ear almost deafened him, as Vincent fired and fired until the hammer clicked on an empty chamber. The car had picked up speed and, in a moment, it was safely out of range.

"We missed!" Incredulity and frustration were in Anthony's voice. "I missed! You missed!"

"No, no!" Vincent insisted. "We did *not* miss!"

"He got away, Vincent! He got away! How could we have missed!" Anthony still could not believe what had happened. "We both missed and he was so close!"

"Listen," said Vincent, "At first I thought we missed, also. But didn't you see? It was as if the shells just bounced off the car! It has a coat of armor. The glass is bulletproof. How can we shoot him, Anthony? How can we kill him?"

It took Anthony Boda several minutes before he could answer the question. They had hurried back to the car and were headed downtown before he spoke.

"I will have Al Karley's life. There's a way. A way that cannot fail."

"And what way is that?" asked Vincent. But Anthony Boda refused to say another word.

They cleaned the guns and put them away and then they returned to Vincent's Restaurant. Lt. O'Hara was sitting at a table, obviously waiting for Anthony.

"I hear you went hunting tonight. You did some shooting up around Southchester."

"Will you have a drink, Lieutenant?" asked Anthony.

"I want you to understand that the game you're after is never in season," said O'Hara. "We have to get him the right way. We're workin' on it day and night. We're putting together the evidence. It's slow but it's sure. And you're the one that started the whole thing."

"Vincent serves a plate of veal here," said Anthony. "Have you eaten your supper?"

"There's no other way," O'Hara continued. "And you can't gun him down. After tonight, he'll have tighter protection. You'll never get to him."

Anthony nodded in agreement. "True. I cannot get to him—but there's a way I can make him come to me—with blood in his eyes, and burning with hatred, and mad with the desire to murder me with his own hands!"

O'Hara thought he had heard it all in his twenty-eight years, but he had never heard anything like this. "What are you trying to tell me, Mr. Boda?"

"And then," said Anthony, calmly, "I shall have the right to kill him. I'll be forced to kill him in self-defense. The veal, Lieutenant. The veal. Let me treat you to a portion of Vincent's delicious veal."

The bus ride upstate was slow—but not unpleasant, and, in any event, Anthony Boda was in no hurry. He had time. Plenty of time. When one's only objective in life is to dispatch another human being to eternity, why rush? He got off at the pretty and picturesque college town with its stately, dignified buildings; its imposing arches and statues. If only he had been born in America, he might have been a student here. If only, he had been able to send Louis. Well, for Anthony, it had been impossible. For Louis, too late. And Louis had been determined to send *his* children. And he would have done it, too, had he lived. He could feel the tears well up in his eyes. Poor Louis. Right or wrong, Louis had wanted no part of the fight. And yet, Louis had to pay the price. The full price. Well. No use thinking about that now. There would be blood for blood.

The white-haired lady behind the desk didn't even look at him twice. He had asked for Miss Karley. He had a package for her. No, he could not leave it. His instructions were to deliver it personally. Well, Miss Karley was not in her room, but he would most likely find her at The Learning Center. He thanked her for the address and her courtesy.

It was then he discovered that, just as there are two sides to a coin, there was also another side to this lovely, little college town. A dark, dismal, ramshackle, filthy side. Tottering, vermin-infested buildings. Garbage scattered all about the street. Hopeless drunks huddled in deserted doorways. The only oasis in this desert slum was a freshly painted, brilliantly lighted store with the sign: "The Learning Center." Evidently, they were about to close for the day. The half-dozen or so fresh faced, expensively-clothed college boys and girls were putting books, papers, and various other learning artifacts, into closets and drawers. He asked for Miss Karley. She was pointed out to him. A beautiful girl. Tall, with long, blonde hair and clear blue eyes. Had her hair been black and her eyes brown, she might have been Anna-Maria at seventeen. He sighed. He was sorry for what he had to do. But there was no help for it.

"Miss Karley?"

"Oh! I'm afraid school's over for the day! Did you have a child you want us to tutor!" Her voice was filled with enthusiasm and excitement. Here was a girl filled with the love of life. He shook his head.

"Oh!" she said. "Well, then, what can I do for you ... Mister Ah...?"

"Boda," he said. "Anthony Boda. Is the name familiar?"

"No. At least, I don't think so," she answered.

"Can we talk in private?" he asked.

"Well ... ah ..." she answered. "There's just the one room." She was becoming just the slightest bit nervous.

"Why don't we sit over there?" He pointed to a bench on the far side of the room. Before she could answer, he took her arm gently. Before she knew what had happened, she was seated.

"Well, what do you want to tell me?" she demanded.

He looked at her. "What do I want to tell you? I want to tell you, that your father, among a thousand other crimes, killed my wife and son."

She gasped. She jumped up to her feet. "Who are you? How dare you! What are you saying!"

He sighed. "You know what I'm saying."

There must be no scene. At all costs, she must not have a scene. "Get out of here," her voice was furious but very low.

"Why?" he asked.

Her pretty face was now twisted with anger. "Get out," she said, through clenched teeth. "Get out before I call a policeman!"

"You will call a policeman?" asked Anthony, quietly. "Why? What have I done wrong. I have only stated a fact."

"You ... you must be mad ...!" But the anger in her voice had changed suddenly to bewilderment.

"Your father, among a thousand other crimes, killed my wife and son," Anthony repeated.

"No. No ...!" She had become a pleading child. "My father ... he ... he's good ... he's kind ... he's the most decent man ... in the world ... his pocketbook is always open to the poor ... he's gentle ... he's ..."

"It's all right, little one," said Anthony Boda. "Talk ... keep talking. Get it all out of your system."

She sat down. She placed her hands over her face.

"You read of it in the paper." Anthony spoke in a low voice. "Anthony Boda, Shoemaker. Remember, his shop was bombed. His wife and son, murdered."

She shook her head. It was a violent movement. "No!" It was a plea of desperation.

"How does your father make his money?" asked Anthony.

"He . . . he . . ." she stopped.

He gave her no chance. "Where is his factory? His store? What goods does he handle? In what does he trade? I'm a shoemaker—I smell of leather. Your father is a murderer. He smells of death!"

"No! No!" There was agony in her voice.

"Tell me what does he do, your father? How does he earn his bread and pay for yours?"

"I . . . I . . ." she could say no more.

He showed her no mercy. "Don't say you don't know. You don't wish to know! You're an American-born girl. Smart. Educated. You read."

Her voice had fallen to a whisper. "Go. Please, go. . . !"

"I suppose it's better not to know. Easier. The money, it bought you so much—raised you so high. But every dollar comes from the gutter. One side is covered with filth—the other is soaked in blood."

Now, the tears were running down her cheeks. She was crying silently, but he knew her heart had just been broken. He patted her shoulder. He would have cried with her, but his own heart had already been broken and there were no more tears. "Crusader chief," he whispered to himself. "All you have done is destroyed the children. Yours and the Infidel's."

And now he must go home and wait for Al Karley.

A week went by. And then, Al Karley had a telephone call from Marissa's roommate that sent him speeding up to the college. When he arrived, the roommate tactfully left them alone. He looked at Marissa's face anxiously. Something was very off with the kid. Her eyes were red. She was thin, pale, nervous. Was she sick? Well, the best doctors would spring into action, the second he picked up the phone.

"Baby, your friend, Enid, she says you just sit around the room day and night. You don't sleep. You forget to eat. Are you sick?"

She turned her face away from him. Something was wrong here. It had to be. But what! "Baby," he said, "is this how you say hello to your old man?"

She stood up. She clasped her hands together. "I have to know something," she said.

"Honey!" he exclaimed. "All you have to do is ask!"

"You remember," she said. "Some time ago. I asked you a question."

He laughed. "Baby, you ask me a million questions!"

162

"I asked you about the man ... in the paper ... and you said it was another Al Karley."

There was a chill wind in the room now. He could feel it becoming colder.

"Was it another Al Karley!" she demanded. "Was it!"

He tried to fight it off. Laugh it off. "Marissa, Honey! What are you trying to ..."

But she wanted the answer, nothing but the answer.

"Don't lie to me, Daddy!" she pleaded. "It's bad enough I had to lie to myself!"

It had happened suddenly, without the slightest hint of a warning, and here he was, fighting for his daughter's love; another way of saying he was struggling for life itself. Yes, it was a moment that had to arrive, but he prayed that it would come when she would be older, much older and, perhaps, he would be dead.

"Tell me!" she demanded, and her voice told him that he was out of time to deny it and there was no longer room to maneuver.

"It was another Al *Karley*," he said quietly. "There are two of us ... two of me. One is your Daddy who loves you more than anything in the world. And the other is ... he's somebody who does what he has to do—the only thing he knows *how* to do!"

Her voice was almost a whisper. "I never saw it

before. But a man—a man named Boda, a shoemaker—he opened my eyes. And I can never close them again."

Boda! The name bit into his brain like the fiery sting of an angry hornet! "Boda!" he shouted. "You said Boda!"

"Yes," she answered. "Boda, Anthony Boda. And I have never seen such dignity, such quiet force in a man. He's the greatest human being I ever met."

Boda! He could feel every pulse pounding, as the hated name swept everything else out of his mind. Now, nothing else existed in the universe but the desire to kill, which could only be satisfied with Anthony Boda's blood. And he would spill that blood with his own two hands. "Boda," he shouted. "I was a fool! I should have made sure of you before! I'll do it now, Boda! I'll kill you now!" He ran out of the room. She started after him. She caught at his arm as he reached the stairs. "No, Daddy! Please!" He thrust her aside. He raced down the steps and out the hall door and into his limousine. She watched the car pull away swiftly, too rapidly for the safety of the campus. But that was the least. She heard what he had said. She understood what he meant. She knew what she had to do. She went back to her room. She picked up the telephone. She asked the operator to connect her with the State Police.

The "bandit" who had been so identified by Anthony Boda as Karley's bodyguard chauffeur the day Al Karley had come to the store, was driving his boss now. He had a name, Benjy. He was accustomed to the idiosyncracies and vagaries of Al Karley's personality and allowed none of them to upset him. This accounted for his longevity on the job. But right now, this thing was definitely getting out of hand. The boss, at all times the coolest of characters, had completely blown his top. The boss was sitting back there screaming, "I'll kill him! I'll kill him! I'll cut his heart out! Floor it! Benjy, floor it!" Benjy knew he must never answer. Never say things like, "That's just what I'm doin', boss." The boss knew the pedal was absolutely jammed against the floorboard. He was only talking to hear his own voice. The limit was sixty. It didn't bother Benjy that they were breaking it. What was a ticket! The problem was, the needle was going past eighty and into ninety and now, ninety-five. And the boss kept screaming, "Floor it, Benjy! Floor it!"

Floor it. Now, the needle kept moving further and further to the right, touching numbers it had never seen before, numbers it was never supposed to meet. A hundred! The thing showed a hundred and twenty, but that was just for show. But here he was at a hundred and five, and moving up. He could hear a shudder in the frame. The car simply was not built to take the speed. Certainly the tires ... it was a hundred and ten! "Floor it, Benjy!"

The shaking was pronounced. It was scary. He decreased the pressure on the pedal. Slowly, the needle moved to the left. Back to a hundred and five. Benjy felt something hard poke at the back of his neck. "Floor it," shouted Karley, "I'll blow your head off!"

It had to be one way or the other. Once again, the needle crawled to the right. For the very first time in almost twenty years, Benjy prayed. Now, above the screaming of the engine, there was an explosive sound and a bump. It was a tire! The hell with Karley! Let him shoot. He took his foot off the accelerator ... but the car began to twist and turn. Now, the wheel just spun away from his hands. There was the terrifying squeal of a high-speed skid and then a jarring, spine-breaking thump that seemed to shake the world loose from its foundations. And then, nothing.

Anthony Boda sat near the window of his apartment. The revolver was close to hand. He was waiting for Al Karley. All week, he had waited. And then, quite suddenly, he discovered he needn't wait any longer. The news had come over the radio. Just a few short words that robbed him of his revenge. A high-speed accident had taken the life of Karley's chauffeur. Karley himself was expected to die at any moment. Slowly, Anthony Boda extracted the shells from the revolver. He wiped the gun carefully and placed it in a cloth bag. Tomorrow morning, he would return the gun to Vincent. Now, he would go to bed and decide how to spend the rest of his life, if, indeed, it was worth spending at all. With that in mind, he considered taking the revolver out of the bag and placing one shell in the chamber. At this point, he really didn't know what he was going to do. He would just sit quietly and let the situation develop. There was a knock on the door. Who could that be? When he had heard about Karley on the radio, he had stopped watching the street. Well, it didn't matter. He heard a voice. It was the police lieutenant.

"Mr. Boda?"

"Come in," said Anthony.

O'Hara opened the door and entered. "You heard the news?" he asked. Anthony nodded.

"His daughter phoned the state cops. He was coming here to kill you."

"Yes," Anthony nodded. "But I have been robbed. I will not have my revenge. He's dead."

"No." said O'Hara. "The driver is dead."

"But Karley is dying," said Anthony. "I heard it."

"Karley doesn't have to die," said O'Hara. "Yes, he did suffer extensive injuries. But he has a chance to recover. The problem is, he has to have a blood transfusion."

"Why is it a problem? He can buy all the blood he needs," Anthony said.

"Well, you'd think so," said O'Hara, "But the fact is, he can't. He happens to have a very rare type of blood."

"Is that a fact?" Boda was genuinely surprised. "I would think his blood is as base and as common as sewage."

The lieutenant shook his head. "He needs a transfusion from someone who has that same rare type. Only someone like that can save him. In the whole city, the whole state, I guess, this whole part of the country, there's only one donor. The hospital has a record of just one person with that exact type." The lieutenant paused. Anthony shrugged. The matter was of absolutely no interest.

"Why tell me this?" he asked.

"Because it's you," said Lt. O'Hara.

Anthony Boda refused to believe it! "I? Me! I have the same blood as that swine!"

"They found out by accident. When you and your ... wife and son ... were brought to the hospital after the ... well, naturally your blood was typed. And one of the lab technicians happened to remember. Anyhow, that's the blood Karley has to have or he'll die before tonight."

Anthony Boda looked closely at Lt. O'Hara. He didn't know whether to laugh or curse! The situation, the turn of events, was simply too much to be comprehended all at once. Finally, he asked, "Do you expect me to give my blood to the murderer of my wife and son? Do you expect I will agree to keep this animal alive?" And then, he decided it was really a joke. He began to laugh.

"Mr. Boda," O'Hara said, "Whatever else this may be, it isn't funny." Anthony Boda stopped laughing. No. It wasn't funny.

"How I prayed," he said. "That I could kill this monster. I thought my prayers would never be answered. But they were. And now, I hold his life in my hands. So you see, Lt. O'Hara, there *is* justice!"

"That's not justice, Mr. Boda. That's revenge."

Anthony nodded. "Well, when a man cannot have justice, revenge is what he must settle for."

"But you can have justice!" O'Hara insisted. "We've built a case. We can put him away. He has to live, to stand trial, so we can break up his rackets. We need your help."

"Where were you when I needed your help, Lieutenant?" Anthony shrugged. "No. Al Karley belongs to me."

"He belongs to all of us. Let the law deal with him. Give him some blood. I'll drive you to the hospital." There was no missing the urgency in O'Hara's voice.

"You can drive me to the hospital. I'm going there, anyhow. But Al Karley will never see one, single drop of my blood!"

"I don't figure this," said O'Hara, puzzled. "Then why do you want to go to the hospital?"

Anthony Boda smiled. But there was no humor in it. Indeed, if he could have seen his face at that moment, he would have noted how closely his eyes resembled those of Chuck Perry. Suddenly, they appeared small and dull. And nothing shone in them.

O'Hara repeated his question. "Why do you want to go to the hospital?"

"To spit in his eye," said Anthony Boda, "to laugh in his face, to let him know who has conquered."

All the way to the hospital in the police car O'Hara kept urging Anthony to change his mind. But Anthony was paying no attention. All that mattered was the confrontation, the delicious moment of confrontation. Who says God never rewards the just? Every dog *does* get his day! Anna-Maria and Louis— they *will* be avenged! The confrontation was hardly what he had expected, though. He had foreseen, a battered and bleeding Al Karley sprawled on blood-stained sheets. What there was, a thin, pinched ravaged face, the head swathed in bandages. Bottles of liquid hanging from stands with tubes leading into various parts of Karley's body. All that seemed alive were the man's eyes. They burned, either with fever or with hope. But there was life in them. Life. He looked down on the man he hated more than anything in the world.

"Can you hear me, Al Karley?"

Karley's lips moved. The voice was weak, but audible.

"Yes . . ."

"Do you know why I came?"

The eyes burned brighter. The lips moved slowly.

"To . . . torture me . . ."

"I was in this hospital," said Anthony Boda. "You killed my wife, my son. I swore I would kill you . . . with my own hands."

"Boda, Boda," the lips were working hard to form the words, "Please . . . please . . . don't let me . . . die . . . Please . . ."

For a moment, Anthony Boda was completely stunned.

"What! What are you saying? You beg me, your sworn enemy for your life . . . !"

"Please," the lips were moving quickly. "let me live, please . . ."

"This! This," exclaimed Anthony Boda! "This is what makes us tremble! This is what owns judges, lawyers, policemen! This is what we fear! You cowardly animal! Can't you even die decently!"

"Please, please, I . . . I . . . never begged from nobody in my life . . . Please . . . Don't let me die!"

"Mr. Boda!" she had run into the room. Her eyes shone.

"Oh, Mr. Boda! You came, you came! I knew you would come! You see, Daddy! I told you Mr. Boda would come! I told you! Mr. Boda is a great man!

Does the doctor know! Have they been told to get ready for the transfusion! Oh, Mr. Boda!"

"The transfusion?" asked Anthony.

"The transfusion" she exclaimed. That's why you came! To give Daddy the blood! Daddy said you'd never do it! Daddy said you would drain every drop of blood from your veins and die first!"

"Shhh!" said Anthony Boda! "A young girl must not talk like that in front of her father. Now, you must say no more."

"I ... I'm sorry," she said. "But, that's what he said."

Anthony nodded slowly. "I know that's what he said. Now, you must excuse us ... you must leave me and your father alone for a little while. Please."

He waited for her to walk slowly from the room. Then he leaned over the bed. His face was very close to Al Karley's.

"Al Karley, can you hear me ...?"

"Yes," Karley whispered.

"Al Karley," said Anthony Boda, "you are very close to Eternity, you know that. So, speak the truth. Speak the truth for the very first time in your life. The truth. Tell me, Al Karley, tell me ... if it were the other way—and I lay dying, would you give me your blood? Answer, and remember, God is listening."

Karley's eyes burned brighter. But his lips remained still.

"The truth, Al Karley, in God's name, the truth. Would you give me your blood?"

Karley's lips began to move. The single word came out.

"No," said Al Karley.

Anthony Boda nodded his head. "Then this is the difference between us. I will give you mine."

Time and Again
or
[The Vampire Clock]

Ian Martin

I, Ethan Vigil, clockmaker by trade, being of sound mind and in possession of all my faculties—knowing that I am about to die—am writing this by my own hand in case, when the moment comes to destroy myself, I fail also to destroy the hourglass clock. For if I fail, someone *must* dispose of it. I mean by that, pulverize it (if they can find a method), bury it, sink it in the bottomless deeps of the ocean, somehow *kill* it—*end* it—before its ghastly existence sucks up in its abhorrent life, God knows how many innocent people, who will die . . . a lingering, unclean, inhuman death, forced upon them to satisfy its fiendish, insatiable thirst. Nor—*let me warn you in the name of God*—let anyone who reads this be trapped by the evil gift this mechanism may offer you. For to accept the special heaven this malevolent engine of the devil holds out, is to become enslaved. To become, at the end, as vile and perverted as the machine itself. . . .

It is very quiet as I write, and the sound of my pen scratches on the paper seems incredibly loud. I suppose that has to do with being almost completely alone for the last time in my life.

I've even stopped all the clocks. Stilled them, as if in some strange propitiation to the one who took over all my life, ruled it, and then destroyed it.

This used to be a magic land for me, filling my ears with the sound of all the different escapements and movements; gravity, spring-induced, electrical impulse: the wealth of chimes that the spinning cogs and wheels activated, the variety of ticks and tocks ranging the whole scale from the bass of the grandfather clocks to the soprano of the cuckoo and the pocket watches.

All my life I have been fascinated (perhaps a better word would be captivated) by the process of time. Oh, not so much its result, but all the devices that measure its passage. Not sundials, you see, or other clocks which use any of a variety of heavenly bodies to isolate time neatly for man. They were functional enough, but they had no life of their own. They didn't hold the mystery and wonder of that magical train of wheels, actuated by a spring or weight or whatever means, and controlled by whatever governing device to establish and regulate the speed so as to make it uniform.

Have you ever owned a clock where the works were clearly in view, or opened up the back of your

178

watch, or a larger clock, to become mesmerized by the perfect precision of the movements? I have studied them all, from the description of the first clock, supposedly built for Pope Sylvester, the second, in 996 down through the quartz and module time-pieces made today. But for all my studies—in all my life (to repeat myself), I had never seen a device the like of which was about to fall into my hands as I begin this history of possession and damnation.

The clock—I have no other special name for it, except perhaps, well, that can wait for later. *The clock* then, as it shall be known for the moment, came to me by complete accident. Just about a year ago, I was working late in my shop, when I heard an insistent tapping at the glass of the door to the street. Normally I would have disregarded it, since my sign, I think, is large (well, I know it is large) and I hope clear enough. It read:

Closed for the night. Set your watch by the timepiece above this sign, and try me at eight in the morning. I'll be there on the dot. Will you?

I was busy at the time and I was closed, so I paid no attention. But the rapping was so insistent, and finally had grown so heavy and imperious, that I was seriously concerned that whoever it was might break the glass.

I pushed back my chair in annoyance, got to my

feet, and crossed from behind my counter towards the entrance door. The damned, insistent idiot outside was still rattling away on the pane. Approaching the door, I called out in some annoyance:

"Stop that! You want to shatter the glass? Can't you see I'm closed up? Can't you read?"

I sound angry as I write these words, but you may believe me, I am a paper tiger. I won't have to convince you—if you continue to read this document I will reveal myself, I'm sure.

The man outside hadn't heard me, but he had seen me approaching the door, and redoubled his assault on the unoffending glass pane.

" 'Elp, guvnor? Please 'elp? Let me in," he howled piteously through the glass.

"I'm closed! Read the sign, and get on with you," I howled back.

"You let me in, and you won't be sorry. Just give *me* the chance, and I'll give *you* the chance *of a lifetime*!"

With a wave of a hand, I was about to turn away from him, when suddenly he stopped me, literally, in my tracks.

It was raining heavily, the water streaming down the glass. The man, himself, was a distorted blur through the screen of water running down the door. Small, and somehow pathetic, huddled in what looked like a worn pea jacket, such as sailors wear. The impression of a sailor was heightened by a battered old peak hat, drawn low over his eyes as if to hide his face. Again, though he was still a half-blur, I had an impression of sleaziness and that this was scarcely a man to be trusted. That's what turned me away from him.

But what turned me back, and held me fascinated, was not the peremptory "Look!" which he had hollered at the top of his voice, but the object which he held close to the glass, and which drew my eyes like a magnet.

It was a clock—the like of which I'd never seen!

Shaped like an hourglass, with a weirdly misshapen pendulum hanging in the lower half, and the face in the upper half lit as though by some strange, inner glow. But what piqued my professional curiosity most of all were the numerals on that strangely illuminated face. For in place of the figure 12 at the top of the dial, was the numeral 13! I had to see that clock more closely!

So, in spite of my earlier better judgment, I opened the door to let in death and deadly destruction!

The moment the door was open, the man himself slid in like some little water rat. I almost expected him to shake himself as an animal does, to get rid of the excess moisture. But instead he cowered nervously, for all the world like that same rat cornered by a cat, his beady little eyes shining and darting from side to side from below the beak of his cap.

"Bless you guvnor. You're a life-saver, you are. All 'eart," he muttered obsequiously. But those eyes were busy all the while ferreting around the shop, assessing, weighing, probing to see if we were alone.

I answered him wryly, and truthfully.

"All heart and no brains. What do you want?"

"I want you to 'ave a look at this 'ere clock!"

His voice was hoarse, and weak, and he seemed to be having difficulty breathing. But for the moment my curiosity was larger than my compassion.

"It's the only reason I let you in," I answered. "I'd like to have a look at it myself."

I had closed the door immediately after he came in to shut out the still-drumming rain, and now I nodded him further in.

"Let's take it over to my workbench," I said.

I waited for him to precede me (I wasn't taking any chances of letting him get at my back), and after a brief hesitation he sort of sloped disconsolately around the end of the counter toward my bench, still clutching the strange clock to him. Then suddenly he stopped, and after a deep breath during which he seemed to have to fight for air, he said:

"You—ah—you wouldn't have a spot of somethin' to take the chill out of a man's bones, would you?"

"You don't ask for much, do you? Force your way into a man's shop after eleven o'clock at night, and then ask him for a drink!" I'm afraid my voice was sarcastic. "I suppose the next thing you'll do is pull out a gun and rob me!"

"Not me, Guv'nor. Not 'Arry Stubbs! I may be down and out, but 'honest's' me middle name." He was having a hard time getting the words out because his teeth were chattering. "I'm 'ere on legitimate business."

I laughed. "Just as well. You wouldn't have gotten much if it wasn't. Not much money in mechanical timepieces anymore. You want that clock repaired?"

"I want to sell it to you, is what I want. I need the money bad, or I wouldn't part with it."

"Put it on the bench and let's have a look at it."

"Y-y-yes, Guv'nor." He coughed suddenly, and I could see his teeth were chattering and he was shaking as if he had malaria. "Could you give me a hand up with it?"

"Here, give it to me," I said. "You're in a pretty bad way!"

"Froze to the marrow and sopping wet," he said, as he relinquished the strange hourglass shape to me. "No way to be, a man with a 'istory of asthma and stuff! I'm not well, not well at all. 'Streuth, so 'elp me. And I'm stony broke an' on the beach."

I knew it could all be an elaborate come-on. But I couldn't help being sorry for the man, and we all only live one life. Enough things have to happen that we'll end up regretting, so what point is there not to avoid the few we can?

183

"I hope I don't regret it," I said, "but come on in the back. To my apartment. There's a fire in the parlor will dry you up some. And," I added as we started back, the clock still in my hands, "Maybe I can find us a drop to take the chill off."

"Bless you, Guv'nor, you're a real gentleman," he said through chattering teeth.

"Or a sucker," I answered, wondering if mine were the teeth that ought to be chattering.

I ushered him through the door into my private apartment in back of the shop, hoping that my sister-in-law Harriet was as safely in bed as I was sure my poor, suffering Henrietta would be at this hour. To my relief the room was empty, and a warm fire was glowing and spitting sparks in the grate.

"In you go," I said. "Better back right up to the fire, and dry yourself out. While you do, I'll put this—this fascinating curiosity on the table, and then see what we can find to wet our whistles."

"That'd be all right, sir."

While he backed up to the fire, I opened up the credenza, for we used this room also for dining. The liquor compartment, as usual, was not very well stocked. I rummaged about among the bottles.

"Let's see . . . Dandelion wine, a sip of sherry, no bourbon." Damn and double damn! Since Harriet came to live with us there seldom is anything worth drinking. Then my eye caught something her eagle eye had missed.

"Aha! Sloe gin! That suit you?"

"I don't know about the slow part, guv'nor. I'm ready to take my tot as fast as I can get it!"

Joke or misunderstanding, it wasn't worth concerning myself about. I got two glasses, opened the bottle, and poured us each a nice stiff shot.

"Want some water?"

"No, Lor' bless you! I'll take it neat. Me outsides are warming up, but inside I'm still as cold as a witch's bustle!"

He lifted the glass in a half-salute, his shaking hand in danger of spilling the neat shot. Then in one quick gulp he downed it. Once the liquor hit his throat, and presumably passed down it, he indulged in a momentary paroxysm of choking. Then, through a rasping breath of relief he got out:

"That's loverly, that is! You're not joinin' me?"

"Be right there. I'm more interested in this clock for the moment." As indeed I was. I couldn't keep my eyes off it. But my companion had a deeper interest. With a fawning, ingratiating tone he begged me:

"Just loverly! Warms the cockles of me 'eart. I don't suppose—?"

I shrugged. "We've gone this far—why not? Help yourself."

"A real gentleman, as I said." He was so eager to pour again he almost spilled it. "Salt of the earth, is the way I'd put it!" He slid a sidelong glance at me, and deciding that I wasn't watching, tipped a little more gin into the glass. Then, quickly, as if he'd never stopped speaking or moved a muscle, "Well—over the 'atch, as a fellow says."

I was too busy to worry about his pettifogging little stratagems to sneak an extra drink. My whole attention was on the incredible, unique masterpiece that he had brought to me. My interest was so strong, that I may have almost snapped the question:

"Where did you get this clock?"

He suddenly turned very cagy, the sharp little eyes flickering up and down under the cap.

"Ah! Well now, Guv'nor, I don't rightly know as I could tell you that, I'm afraid."

"But you're not afraid to try to sell it to me. How do I know it's yours?"

"Oh, it's mine all right," he said hastily. "I mean I've got it, haven't I?" Then as he judged that argument would hardly suffice, he changed to the wheedling tone again. "You might say it came into my possession, d'ye see, when its owner died." And then expansively, as the liquor began to take hold. "You might say it was *willed* to me."

He was such an obvious little toady that, even though perhaps I should have been afraid I wasn't, as I snapped at him, saying:

"Or, you might say, you stole it!"

"Not me! Never 'onest' 'Arry Stubbs. Ask anyone as knows me!"

"Since you're obviously English and here we are in America, I'm not very likely to meet anyone that does, am I?"

"Now that's God's truth, sir, me bein' from t'other side of the Atlantic." He lowered his voice to a clumsy misterioso on this next: "Which is where this 'ere clock comes from. So you wouldn't 'ave to worry about its bein' stolen, wot with the distance and the owner bein' dead." The little eyes were busy scurrying across my face like startled ants. But never for a moment did they stop weighing, assessing, trying to decide how effective whatever he said was. "Not that it *was* stolen, Guv'nor. Oh no, not likely, not bloody likely, perish the thought, there! No, I got it, d'ye see, in payment for a debt of honor. Sort of accounts receivable, as you might say." He was watching me very carefully now.

"Accounts receivable?" I questioned with an eyebrow and my tone of voice. "Then it's working, I mean it's in running order, this clock?"

For a brief moment we were measuring each other. But quickly, Harry Stubbs was his chameleon-like self, changing in midstream, sliding away from the direct question, while he changed his colors to fit the new situation. Suddenly he was all open frankness, spreading his arms in a gesture of giving, revealing his browned and rotting teeth in what he must have supposed to be an ingratiating smile.

"I'm glad you brought it up, Guv'nor. For I can

give you proof you're dealin' with a man o' his word when you deal with 'Arry Stubbs. I wouldn't tell a gentleman like you no lie! No sir. No, most definitely not!" He shook his head in a parody of a man of total probity giving an honest appraisal. "That there clock, *it don't run*! I'd be the first one to admit that. 'Asn't run, for a fact, since the old man died."

"What old man?"

"The old man what I—," he suddenly bit off whatever had almost slipped out, looking crafty again. "What I mean is, the old cove I 'ad business with 'oo owed me—well—certain things. He was the one gave it me."

"He was in the clock repairing business?"

I was answered by a hoarse, but full chuckle from Harry Stubbs.

"Lor' love a duck, no! Pawnbroker, 'e was." He suddenly became very confidential, practically taking me by the lapel and delivering each word as if in between the sentences he ought to keep a lookout over his shoulder.

"I went there—Bristol, England this was—to pick up me father's watch that had been left in pawn. Ticket an' everything, though it was a few years it 'ad sat there. And Blimey, if 'e 'adn't sold it on me. Coo lummy, I was 'ot under the collar, an' I let 'im 'ave it, you trust me for that. Well, 'e come right back at me, givin' as good as 'e was gettin', and right in the middle of the argument, he up and dies on me! Well, me ship was sailin', I didn't want to get mixed in nothin' like that, might keep me ashore an' all, so I puts me money on the counter an' looked about. This 'ere machine caught me eye, I dunno just why, so I grabbed it an' got out of there as fast as I could. Like I said, I dunno why ... it just sort of caught me eye. Sw'elp me God, that's the 'ole story."

As if to corroborate this impassioned statement he swept off his peaked cap in one dirty, little hand, and spread his arms as if defying justice, or any supreme being, to question any part of his tale. If I'd been less interested in the clock, I suppose I might have thought him at worst pathetically amusing, particularly since as he removed his cap, it had twisted the thin hair of his head up to a little point so that he looked like a begrimed kewpie doll, or perhaps a dishevelled leprechaun. But the man himself, as I said, interested me little, so all I replied, somewhat dubiously I suppose, was:

"Why, with a whole pawn shop open to you, would you pick up a clock? Particularly one that wouldn't run?"

His eyes narrowed, and he screwed up his wizened weatherbeaten face as if thinking was a difficult job for him.

"Now there's the 'ole point, d'ye see," he said. "I 'ad my eye on this 'ere, from the very beginning. I don't know why, but it just took me fancy the moment I went in. And mark you, it *was* runnin' then. I know, because, while I was talkin' to the old man, I couldn't take my eyes away from it, the peculiar shape and all, and that thirteen there instead of twelve, and during the time I was there (till the old man up and died) I saw the minute 'and click over several times."

"And when did it stop running?"

"Search me, Guv'nor. By the time I made ship it 'ad stopped. An' I couldn't find no way to start 'er up again."

"I see," I said slowly, watching him, and thinking. "And what would you consider a clock like this is worth?"

He licked his lips carefully. Then, with a great display of close camaraderie, he leaned toward me confidentially. From the smell of liquor on his breath I could tell mine wasn't the first drink he'd had.

"Whilst we make a bargain on that," he suggested hoarsely, " 'ow's for sharin' another little spot?"

"I haven't even drunk mine yet," I pointed out mildly.

He seized on that and turned it into an offer to cajole another one. "Just wot I say," he said. "You wouldn't want to be drinkin' alone while we settle a bargain between gentlemen. Man to man like?"

I had a sudden vision of what my sister-in-law Harriet's reaction would be if she came down and found me whooping it up with such an unprepossessing character. Not that Harriet was so prepossessing—just *possessive*. Sometimes I seem to be even more married to her than to her sister, my real wife, Henrietta. But this was only a random, vagrant thought, far away in the back of my mind. In the foreground was my fascination with this queer and unusual mechanism sitting on my dining room table.

"Very well," I agreed. I poured him another drink. "Now, before you drink. Name your price."

His eyes squinted craftily, but they were also straying hungrily to the fresh drink in my hand.

"Well," he said, "I was thinking of—ooh say—around two 'undred and fifty pounds!" Then quickly as he caught my expression he amended that. "Just with the exchange wot it is, Guv'nor, you know. Say just whatever amount over two 'undred would bring it up to, like a thousand American dollars, eh?"

His quick change hadn't altered my reaction. "Nonsense!" I said. "It's a very old mechanism, probably irreparable and—" I fastened him with my eyes, "of questionable ownership." That shook him all right. "I'll give you twenty dollars."

He assumed a pained expression. "Now look 'ere—"

"There isn't much money in clock repairing anymore," I interrupted him before he could say any more, "and my shop is a bit out of date. I happen to have a little personal cash which I have saved." I

191

sighed as I dug it out of my left hip pocket, where I kept it hidden from the distaff side of my household. "Forty-five dollars is all I have. You can take it or leave it."

He had suddenly grown very haughty under the influence of his drinks, since he was no longer shaking: "Well now, I'm afraid not, Mister 'ooever you are. 'Arry Stubbs is no fool! 'E knows a good thing when he sees it. I may be down and out, but I 'ave no intention of being taken advantage of by a—"

"I don't think there's any question who's being taken advantage of here!"

At that rasping, piercing feminine voice we both whirled around. My sister-in-law was standing on the lower step of the staircase to upstairs and the bedroom area.

"Harriet!" I gasped weakly. Mr. Stubbs hadn't anything to say. He hadn't as yet been exposed to the 160 lbs. of wobbling fat that comprises the 5' 2" frame of the sheer, unadulterated bitch who is my wife's only relative. Best thing you can say for Harriet is it isn't her fault the way she looks outside. The Lord knows she tries hard enough to fix that with creams and curlers and astringent mud under the eyes and false lashes and who knows what else! Trouble is, she should work just as hard on the way she is *inside*, because maybe there she might be able to make an improvement. Only thing is she never will. Yes, you have to admit it. Harriet is just an ugly woman inside or out!

"Who is this person, Ethan?" she asked me.

"Why Harriet, he's a customer, more or less," I answered. Then I turned to Stubbs who was regarding this vision in hair curlers, Doctor Denham pajamas, and an old flannel bathrobe. "Mr. Stubbs, this is my sister-in-law—"

And that's as far as I got before Harriet, acting as if she was in coronation robes with a tiara on her head, or a halo round it, cut me down:

"I don't need any introduction to a person of this type. He's certainly not the kind of customer we need in *our* store from what I overheard coming downstairs. Especially now that I see him. Tracking all this mud and grime into a living room which may I remind you *I* have to clean!"

I mean when Harriet looks down her nose she looks *down*! I didn't hold any particular brief for Stubbs, but I did feel she was coming on a bit strong so I protested a little weakly:

"Now, wait a minute, Harriet—"

"I have no intention of waiting, Ethan Vigil! And you should be ashamed to keep my poor, sick sister waiting! In all her pain and misery she needs her husband to bring her a little faith and consolation.

I had no desire to talk about my wife's infirmities in front of a stranger, so I searched for a suitable reply. But with Harriet there never really is a suitable reply. Relief came from a strange quarter. Harry Stubbs pulled himself together, and with a strange mixture of injured pride and a kind of cringing apology, managed with some degree of dignity to say:

"Well now, Ma'am, I certainly would be the last 'un to intrude on family problems. Nevertheless I—"

Harriet was not one for any fancy sword play. Her style was cut and thrust.

"Then don't!" she said succinctly.

Having delivered her ultimatum, she naturally turned to someone else to carry out the royal command.

"Ethan," she continued, "Get rid of this man! How you ever let a stranger in to the house at this time of night, the streets and the city being the way they are, is beyond me. Why, we could all have been murdered in our beds!"

I had to protest that one.

"Heaven's sakes, Harriet," I said mildly, "Let it be!" And then to the object of all this excitement: "You'd better go."

"But what about our business? What about the clock?"

"I've given you my best offer. Forty-five dollars is all I have to my name!"

For a moment he was ready to protest, and then with one wary eye on Harriet and a more greedy one on the cash in my hand, he made a sudden decision.

"I'll take it!" he said.

"Don't you do it, Ethan!"

"Oh, mind your own business for once, Harriet!" It snapped out of me like a spring released, before I realized that for once Ethan Vigil, the worm, had turned. I tried to keep a smug little grin from spreading over my face at Harriet's amazement. Instead, I just enjoyed the warm glow inside. There's nothing like a little lese majesté to give a man's soul a hitch up the ladder.

But for once, and perhaps the only time in my life, I should have listened to Harriet. I should have let that nagging, dominating sister-in-law of mine run my business as usual. Only I didn't.

And because of it we were all doomed.

Not that I had the slightest suspicion of that at the time. I was riding a personal crest. The desire to own the strange clock, more overpowering and overwhelming than any in my experience, was an obsession. I couldn't wait to be alone with it. To take it apart, examine it piece by piece, unit by unit, study and discover whatever principle made it operate.

Oh, I had little doubt that my sailor friend, who called himself Harry Stubbs, had questionable title to its ownership. Under normal circumstances—I consider myself an honest man—I would have had no part of what might be stolen goods. But like all collectors, the terrible urge to own something totally and unreservedly unique is an overriding passion. How many souls have sold themselves as easily to the devil under the same spell?

So I gave Harry Stubbs the money, had him scribble a receipt I was reasonably sure wasn't worth the paper it was written on, and, with a still-dumbfounded Harriet looking on, escorted him through the shop, and passed him through my shop door, out of my life forever.

When I came back into the living room, Harriet was waiting to accuse me. "Is he gone?"

"Yes."

"Good riddance. Be sure to turn out all the lights! Then you get back upstairs to Henrietta!"

"I still have some repair work to do," I tried to temporize.

"Which you should have finished, instead of getting involved with that disreputable tramp. Now don't you move away from me for a moment."

"I'm not moving, that I know of." I answered her quietly, but as usual she was making my blood boil. What I should have said was:

"Who cares what you have to say!"

"What'd you say, Ethan?"

"Nothing special, Harriet. Just what is it *you* want to?"

"First of all, close the doors tight and lock up. Way the world today is, not a one of us is safe."

"From what?"

"Robbery, murder, rape, and just plain carelessness!"

"What's that?"

"Just look at this room after you had that—that derelict in here! A room I break my back keeping clean and neat for you and my poor twin sister! Not only that, lights on all over the place eating up money. To say nothing of good, hard cash thrown away on that piece of trash on the table."

I had to protest that. "It was my own money!" I said.

"What own money?" Harriet retorted with shrewish scorn: "What own money? Why, you and Henrietta wouldn't have a roof over your heads, let alone a place of business, if it wasn't for me! It's my money as well as hers keeps you going, and don't you forget it!"

As if Harriet ever would let me! And, in a sense she was right, which was what made it so difficult ever to answer. Even though I tried:

"But Harriet—"

"I don't want to hear any more! Henrietta is pining away for you. She's sick and helpless, but instead of being with her, you—"

"I was only down here in the shop trying to catch up on repairs!"

197

"Don't try to be clever, Ethan. You were down here trying to avoid your real responsibilities. But you can't escape them. Upstairs with you."

"I'd like to have another look at this clock before I do."

"You'll waste no more time, or light, or fuel down here tonight!"

Harriet had regained her composure, and was charging again like the Light Brigade.

"If it wasn't for good money paid out," she continued, "I'd take that piece of junk on the table and dump it in the rubbish! Now let's get up to bed!"

How I wish I'd listened to her. Just dumped that fiendish clock in the garbage and let the city collect it with the morning trash and bury it forever! But Fate hadn't planned it that way, and the habit of living with two demanding women—each in her own way—had long ago turned me into a weak reed that bent with whatever storm was blowing. Why are we so stupid? Why didn't I realize I was the storm center of a tornado that I never dreamed would suck me up in its vortex?

Since I didn't I succumbed, obediently as usual, to Harriet and climbed upstairs to face my one-time bride, Henrietta, my ailing wife, who was a problem that I didn't know how to solve either.

As always, I cracked the lock on the door, carefully and reasonably professionally, like a professional. But Henrietta was waiting for me. At the slightest sound she activated her frail tentacles and reached out to me in the plaintive invalid's voice:

"Ethan? That you?"

"Yes, Henrietta."

"Where have you been?"

"Working dear. Are you hurting?"

"When don't I hurt?"

"I don't know. How's your back?"

"It isn't my back, this time. It's my stummick. Ethan, I'm scared!"

"Now, Henry, no reason to be—"

"I've been afraid to think of it. But now I'm sure Harriet's right! She's sure that I've got the—"

"Hush! None of that. You just get off to sleep. That's what you need!"

"Well, you better come right to bed and join me, or I won't sleep a wink!"

"Yes, Henny dear."

"I know it's a chore and a burden to have a sick wife to bear."

"Now, Hennie, have I ever complained?"

"Maybe not. But you just don't know how it is to be sore and suffering every blessed minute of every day. I just wonder why the good Lord picked me out to carry this heavy load!"

As I slipped under the covers a minute or two later, and lay wide awake, with Henny snoring away beside me, I have to admit that the same thought crossed my mind. As it had so many nights, no matter how hard I tried to fight off the notion. Because I was ashamed at the selfishness of it, since I was questioning God for *my* share of the burden, not Henny's.

But tonight, the nagging, bitter thought lingered only briefly. Instead, my mind went back to my purchase, to that strange clock on the living-room table downstairs, to the intriguing mystery of a mechanism I had never even imagined in forty years of clockmaking. *And most of all to the enigma of why 13 replaced the numeral 12 on the face.*

For a long time I lay sleepless, dwelling on it, puzzling over it, driven to get up and go down and examine it, but afraid to move, lest I disturb Henrietta, or even worse, Harriet. And at last, nature took over and my eyes began to droop.

The last thing I remember consciously was trying desperately to remember exactly what the irregular shape of that curious weight on the pendulum reminded me of, but just when I thought it might be coming to me, I fell asleep.

I was up with the lark, but I couldn't steal a march on Harriet. Harriet had an axe to grind, and when that woman got out her whetstone, nobody, least of all me, escaped the sparks. She laid into all through breakfast about letting undesirables into the house, exposing two good women to death and destruction! And the Lord knows, even worse, drinking, wasting hard-earned money on trash! *And* my voting record! I don't really know what that had to do with the rest of it, except whenever I was getting coals heaped on my head, it always turned up. I never ceased to wonder if it might not have upset her so much if I'd just voted Democrat. Oh, I'd have heard about that all right, but somehow I get the notion it was the *Independent* that really stuck in her craw. Harriet liked to rule her own little roost, having not much else to do, and she didn't take much to insubordination in the pecking ranks. Fortunately, she couldn't object to my going to work, and that won me at least temporary freedom.

All that morning, between my infrequent customers, I puzzled and poked and pried to reveal the workings of that bizarre clock. But it defied all my efforts. Just before lunchtime, I was completely stymied, when suddenly my wife surprised me by coming out to the bench in her bathrobe over her nightgown.

With all the clocks ticking away, and my absorption in my mystery one, I didn't hear Hennie till she spoke:

"Ethan!"

"Henny," I answered, with a start. "I didn't hear you come in. What's wrong?"

"Where's Harriet?"

"Why, I suppose she went to market."

"I've been calling and calling for someone!"

201

"I'm sorry, dear," I said apologetically. "Like I said, I didn't even hear you come in."

"Oh you! You can't hear anything over this click-ety-clack," she said petulantly. Her face looked drawn, and she seemed on the verge of tears. I didn't want her to start crying. You don't know what it's like when Henny starts crying. After long experience I've learned the best way to cheer her up about her problems is to get her talking about them. That way she seems to be *happy* about them instead of *sad*.

"Is it your back again, dear?" I asked solicitously.

"No it isn't my back," she replied. "It's my head. I've got one of those blinding headaches again. I think we should send for Dr. Royce."

Quite frankly, I didn't. Jake—Dr. Jacob Royce—is my oldest and dearest friend. Come to think of it, I guess, my only one. And I knew Jake doesn't take to house calls, particularly to one of this kind. So I delayed.

"Couldn't it wait until tonight, sweetheart? Jake's coming over for our weekly chess game and—"

"Oh, of course. Why not? I don't want to bother anyone." She was laying the sarcasm on with a trowel. "Far be it from me to complain, even though I am at death's door!"

Well, I'd asked for it. I had turned on the complaint factory, and although I seem to have a genius for pressing the right button for *that*, I never have learned what button there is—if any—to turn it off again! I tried to back-pedal by saying:

"Now honey, if you're really sick—"

That was a total mistake!

"If I'm really sick!"

She rolled her eyes expressively in the general direction of Heaven, as if to make sure that anyone watching up there would understand, and agree with her, that Man with a capital 'M' didn't have a sympathetic bone in his body. I guess that must have been the rib he gave away to Woman. At the same time, she gave a sort of snuffling, helpless laugh that expressed how hopeless it all was to try to explain to anyone so obtuse. And the coup de grâce was that last line delivered with a kind of medium dudgeon, that was *guaranteed* to reduce me to abject apology. She got it.

"Henrietta—darling—please! If it's important—"

No queen ever dismissed a subject so trivial with more grandeur. Her voice fairly throbbed with patient resignation.

"If anyone can suffer in silence, I can."

It was the clock that saved me. For at this moment Henny's eye fell on it, and she moved to look at it more closely. Her lip curled, and her nose gave a little rabbit sniff of disdain.

"Is that the old clock Harriet told me about this morning? The one you threw away hard-earned money on?"

I defended it very carefully.

"Now Henny. It's a very valuable antique. An original! And after all, it was my money."

"Does it run?"

"No."

"Then what good is it?"

"Well, it's certainly worth the forty-five dollars I paid for it. At the very least. In working condition, it could be priceless!"

She eyed it dubiously, her nose twitching again. What I call Henny's is-something-burning? look.

"*Can* you fix it?" she challenged.

"I don't know."

"Why not?"

"Because I've never in my life seen anything like it!"

In spite of my candor and my doubts, looking at the clock I had this feeling, this absolute knowledge inside me, that some way or other I was going to make that clock run! And my enthusiasm began to build up inside me in reverse proportion to Henrietta's disenchantment.

"What's it made of? Feels like some kind of cheap, thin leather."

"No. It's thinner than any leather I can think of. Almost like—" I hesitated for a moment, not quite sure how to express it. "Well, like I don't know what. Parchment maybe. Or—"

As I hesitated, Henny took me up on it, forcing my answer.

"Or what?"

"It's a rather wild fancy, Henny. Maybe it's that hourglass shape, but—" Again I stopped, faintly embarrassed. Henny was in no mood to coddle me. She almost snapped it out:

"For pity's sakes, Ethan, get it out, whatever it is you're trying to say!"

"It's only I feel kinda foolish, but you see the form the, ah, the material is stretched over."

"I may be a sick woman but I am not blind."

"Well, whatever *that's* made of, it's neither wood, nor metal, nor plastic. Something more like horn. Or bone."

"Bone?"

"I think that's what made the connection in my mind. *Skin and bone*. Just run your hands over it again. Doesn't it feel like you imagine cured human skin might feel?"

Henny's first answer was a derisive snort. Her second:

"Sometimes you are a caution. You have too many wild fancies to be a real down-easter. Cured human skin indeed! Some kind of poly-whatever-you-call-it is all. It's an ugly-enough-looking thing whatever it's made of. What's inside it?"

"That's the whole problem. I haven't found the way to get there yet."

"Isn't there someplace in the back to open it?"

"Nope."

"Then how about these glass doors—or windows—or whatever they are in the front?"

"They're not hinged. There's no spring rim. I don't know how to get them out."

"If you have to, you could break them."

"No Henny. Whatever they're made of, there doesn't seem to be any way to break them."

Henrietta was as bored with this conversation as I was interested. Her voice began to take on a tart edge just a little less sharp than a razor blade.

"Oh Ethan, let's stop diddling around. There *has* to be a way to get at the works. Or to try to make it go. Have you tried shaking it."

"What for?"

"Why, to get that funny-looking pendulum ticking, or swinging, or whatever it's supposed to do."

"That's one of the troubles, Henny. It doesn't seem to be the way it's activated. It's some different principle."

I lifted the clock and shook it, my hand spanning its hourglass waist. For a weird moment I had a feeling as though it wasn't an object, but somehow a minute human being, and a very feminine one at that. But this was the merest, fleeting impression next to my concentration on the extraordinary machine.

"Look at the pendulum," Henrietta said. "It's all

lopsided. It must have started to melt or something."

"I don't think so," I answered. "I have a feeling it was made that shape for a reason."

"What reason?"

"Don't I wish I knew!"

"I think it's just melted, or falling apart. Can't you get inside and find out?"

"That's the whole problem, Henny."

"You mean there's no way of repairing it?"

"There *must* be a way."

"How do you get into the works?"

"Only through this tiny little lid on the top."

As I opened it, the same phenomenon happened that I had noticed every time I had opened it before. There was a tiny, protesting shriek, less like metal binding against metal than like an animal voice.

"Why don't you oil it, Ethan?"

Sometimes I have momentary blinding rages for no reason, when I see red, like blood, behind my eyes. I never do anything about them. It seems to be some sort of defense mechanism for me to blow away stupidity and my own frustrations, like a vigorous broom and scrubbing spree among attic cobwebs. There certainly was no trace of passion in my quiet reply.

"Don't you think that's the first thing someone in my trade would do, Henny? It doesn't seem to make any difference. No matter how I try to lubricate it,

I can't get that squeak out. Now, go ahead, look in if you want."

She did so, and I had to move my head quickly to avoid having one of my eyes removed by her curlers. As she peered, head cocked on one side (for indeed the opening was so small you really had to examine the interior with one eye or the other), I mused idly to myself when the last time was that I had seen Henny's hair out of curlers. It occurred to me that I couldn't quite remember how she wore it normally.

"Is that all you can see of the insides?" she asked.

"That's right," I explained. "I can't even tell what the gears, the pinions, and the axles are made of. With a clock this age, they should be wood. But they look more like horn, or bone to me."

"Can't you lift the whole movement out to see?"

"No possibility of that. The opening is so small I can't even get my hand in there to feel."

"That's ridiculous," Henrietta snorted. "If you can't . . . I can."

She took her head away, and rolled back the sleeve of her gown. Then, her eyes on me in a sort of triumphant you're-so-silly-you-can't-do-anything-without-me look, she introduced her hand into the small opening, and gradually maneovered it into the works.

All of a sudden she let out a small gasping scream and withdrew her hand quickly. There was a minute crimsoning drop of blood on one finger.

"Look at what your silly old clock has done!" she said to me accusingly.

"Let me see."

"My finger. It's bleeding." She was biting her lip and pouting against tears like a little child. "It felt like something bit me!"

I tried to be reassuring and sympathetic and not sound like it was a ridiculous fuss over nothing.

"Let me see, sweetheart." And then as I examined it. "Oh, it's just a small scratch."

"Just the same I'm not taking any chances with that dirty old clock. I could end up with blood poisoning!"

She pulled her hand away from me and started out of the shop for our apartment in the back.

"I'm going to run this under water. Now you get me a bandage and disinfectant right away so I can sterilize this."

Her voice had faded, cut off by the closing door. I suppose I must have assented automatically to whatever Henrietta was saying, but I wasn't conscious of that.

What I was conscious of, was a sudden realization that grabbed and held all my interest as I realized that from the moment Henrietta had made her small yelp of pain—

The clock had started to run!

There was no mistaking the fact that this dead timepiece had somehow come to life! It had started to record time again, in its own peculiar way. How could I tell? Because the pulsation of whatever power chain drove it, was totally different from the mechanical ticks and tocks of all the other myriad clocks upon my wall. This was an individual rhythm, not to be confused with any of them, for this was a sound akin—if not completely similar—to the beat of the human heart!

Whatever my wife had accidentally touched, the clock now remained running steadily. Loath as I was to leave it, I followed Henny into the back, got her some disinfectant, and having ascertained that all she had was the merest scratch, sterilized and bandaged it, and left her with a sigh of relief to lie down a little because she was feeling dizzy.

Back in the shop, I hastened eagerly to the clock. On an impulse, I went to the street door and turned the sign indicating that I was closed, and closed the lock. I paused only for a second to give my avocado tree in the window a drink of water, and then, eagerly, returned to my bench. The clock was still running.

Examining it as I did made this curious chronometer even more of an enigma. Peering down through the lid behind the face, I could just make out the gears behind the face that minute by minute, second by second, operated the hands that spelled out the time. What motivated them was obvious: the strange mass in the lower half of the hourglass that I had mistakenly thought a pendulum. Now, quite clearly, it was nothing of the kind. It was not a weight, designed to swing back and forth. Quite clearly it operated on a totally different principle. A principle that made me gasp in sheer surprise as I understood it at last.

This was a diaphragm, or a pump, opening and closing to create energy, in a motion like the human fist clasping and unclasping or—

Yes, I suddenly knew why its irregular shape was so familiar. This was in every essence a facsimile of the human heart!

But what in turn motivated that, or fueled it, was the ultimate mystery. That process was locked away in the belly of the clock, somewhere between those transparent windows, hidden from all human sight until one could dismantle the whole thing somehow or other.

Meanwhile, everything about this clock was different. Exotic Strange. Even its chime for the hours was outré, a plangent, plaintive sound that echoed the human voice.

An old customer came by for whom I *had* to open the door. I hurried him out as fast as I could, but business suddenly picked up, and my attention, in spite of myself, had to be diverted from the clock. Oh, I kept checking it! It drew me irresistibly all afternoon long, and even after dinner, while I

211

waited for Dr. Royce to come and check up on my wife.

While he was seeing Henrietta, I laid out our chessboard, but with none of my usual interest and anticipation. My gaze kept wandering to the enigmatic clock, which was still pulsing strongly away.

Oh, I suppose nobody else could have heard it among all the busy sounds of my regular army of clocks, but to me, used as I was to their mechanical measures of time, all I could hear was that strange pulse beat, so different from all of them.

I was just setting up our chairs, and pushing Jake's ashtray for his cigar into place automatically, my mind on the clock, when Jake startled me.

I hadn't heard him come in. I probably wouldn't have noticed King Kong if he'd blundered in just then.

Let me just digress a moment to tell you about Jake. He's a small, spare man, where I am getting a little rotund. You could say that Jake is like a bird, as long as you meant any kind of tough bird, not a predator, but capable of taking care of himself. A woodpecker, maybe, or a wren. A no-nonsense guy. Kind, understanding, but pragmatic. He could believe in dreams, but not illusions, particularly any where a person is fooling himself. Lonely—like me. And a hell of a good chess player. Poker too. We're pretty much alike, I reckon, except he never married and I did.

"What the devil are you doing out here, Ethan?"

As he came into the shop from the back, his voice had that harsh, peremptory sound that scared all his patients into paying attention. I knew his bark was not only worse than his bite, but he didn't have any bite at all. He was a sentimental old geezer under all that bluster. So I wouldn't ever give him any satisfaction by bridling under his tone. I just answered mildly:

"Sorry Jake. Just monitoring this clock. Got me mesmerized. How's Henrietta?"

"What am I going to tell you, Ethan?"

"Same thing as usual?"

"Yep. Not a trace of any somatic problem. Never is. Vital signs; all functions, normal."

With a kind of wry apology he made a vague gesture round and round with his first finger near his temple.

"It's all upstairs. Only that's not completely fair. It isn't any real, full-fledged psychiatric problem."

"But damn it, Jake, she has enough pains in enough places to stock a hospital ward. There's got to be something wrong!"

"Oh, there is, there is. But I'm afraid it's incurable, Ethan."

"You don't mean a cancer?"

"Oh, no. Something a lot more prevalent than even that dread disease. I'll give you a name for it, if it's any help. Won't be any cure. Chronic inadequate.

213

Someone who just can't handle the simple process of life, and has to make up excuses for his deficiency. Or in this case, hers."

"There's nothing you can give her for it?"

"Ethan I've been trying to for thirty-odd years. Now—" he shrugged and sighed with a rueful smile, "I've just plain run out of pills, placebos, and pep talks. I'm sorry."

"Why Jake, I know you did your best?"

"I didn't mean that, old chum. I'm sorry for *you*."

I didn't know how to answer that, but I did have a feeling of what I ought to do, even though I knew it wouldn't do much good. I'd tried my remedy which also began with a "p." Just good old-fashioned prayer. But it hadn't made any change in the way things were.

"I'd better go to her," I said. Jake shook his head quietly, and clapped me on the shoulder.

"No need," he assured me. "If I couldn't do anything for Henrietta, there was something I could do for you. I gave her a sedative. Won't hurt her, but it might do you some good. Come on, I'll prescribe for you. What we need is a right smart game of chess."

For once I didn't want to play. I wanted to get back to the clock. But I couldn't disappoint my old friend. I decided not even to show it to him, or get distracted by it. It wouldn't be fair. Jake doesn't share my passion for clocks and their workings. I guess I can understand that. Still, when you come to think of it, we've both spent our lives studying machines; though I guess I'd have to admit the human body's a bit more complex and a lot more efficient than even the finest clock movement. So, anyway, I accepted Jake's prescription and moved to the chessboard.

"I set us up out here," I said, "All right with you?"

He looked around him with a sour expression.

"With all these damn machines whirring, and wheezing, and squawking, and striking? Who can concentrate?"

"I have a sort of patient here, I want to keep my eye on, Jake."

He slid a myopic glance at my new acquisition with sublime disinterest.

"Another of your lame ducks," he said, and added a sardonic, grumphing laugh. "You're a born martyr, Ethan. If you can't sit up with one sick body, it's got to be another." Then he laughed, and poked me in the side. "Just joking. Okay, my masochistic friend, I will suffer the tortures of this cacophony of clock cadences, if you'll spare me any recital of the symptoms of your sick friend there, and let us start the game. I get enough from the human ding-dongs to frazzle my brain. What do I need from a sick clock? I want to forget anything that moves except pawns, bishops, knights, rooks, and so on."

He sighed as he sat down.

"A little peace is all I ask. I guess it's all most human beings ask in the long run. Which reminds me. Where's the main harpy?"

"You mean Harriet?"

"Who else?"

"She had a toothache. She went to bed early."

"Good!" He chuckled to himself with relish, and added: "On both counts! I can't think of anyone who deserves a toothache more, and since it's almost midnight, I was afraid she might come whistling in on her broomstick! Sleep tight, Harriet . . ."

He had picked up a pawn of each color in each fist, and he now extended both hands to me.

"Pick a fist and let's get started."

I indicated his right hand and he opened it. He chortled in delight.

"Black," he said, "I'm glad I start. I have a new wrinkle on the king's pawn opening that's going to lay your ears back."

I grinned back at him. The old companionship always started to ease the strain I lived under without knowing it.

"After all these years? I'd just like to see that."

"You're going to, my boy, you're going to."

Then as he realized that, unconsciously, my eyes had strayed to the clock to satisfy myself that it was still running, he added:

"Come on. Let's forget that damn clock and get down to serious business!"

So (*for the last time*), I forgot the clock. I say for the last time, because it was destined to haunt the rest of my days. We hunched over the chessboard, completely absorbed in the game.

AND ALL THE WHILE, INEXORABLY, AS WE DID SO, ALL THE CLOCKS CONTINUED TO SPELL OUT THE TIME, TICKING STEADILY ON TOWARDS THE FIRST TWELVE O'CLOCK SINCE THE MYSTERY CHRONOMETER STARTED RUNNING. AND THE STUNNING REVELATION IN EXPLANATION OF WHY THAT NUMBER 13 DOMINATED THE CLOCK FACE WAS ABOUT TO BE MADE BY THE CLOCK ITSELF.

"Don't think much of your King's pawn variation, Jake," I was just saying as all my clocks began to strike the hour, each a little out of synchronization with the other.

Jake was chuckling and rubbing his hands together.

"You ain't seen nothing yet, boy. Got you boxed in. Your move."

"Don't rush me. I'm thinking. I'm thinking."

Jake swivelled his head to glare angrily at the inoffensive clocks.

217

"God in heaven, how can you? With that infernal racket going on?"

"What racket?" I said, and then realized. "Oh, the clocks striking? Don't even notice them any more I'm so used to them. There, that's my move. Go on—go ahead, or are you ready to give up?"

"Course not! But who can think of a chess move with all hell breaking loose? From now on we start our games *after* midnight. It's enough to drive a man stark staring mad."

Through Jake's reaction, I had become conscious of all the clocks myself, and I could sympathize with him, though I wasn't about to let him know that. With new ears I was listening to their staggered cacophony, which was now building to a climax. Very few clocks can be made to keep perfect time. The early ones, running a little fast, were now being joined by the more accurate, and the beginning of the chimes from the ones running slower. It *was* quite an avalanche of sound. Jake wanted one last word on the subject:

"I swear to Sam Hill, Ethan," he said, "that you delib—"

The word was snipped off in the middle, as neatly as if it been cut in half with a razor-sharp machete. For at that exact instant the hourglass clock had chimed just once!

And with its chime every other sound in the world had ceased to be!

THE SUDDEN SILENCE WAS DEAFENING. SAVE FOR THE BEAT OF THE CLOCK, AND MY OWN HEART, THE UTTER LACK OF SOUND WAS PETRIFYING! A GOOD WORD, PERHAPS, FOR NOT ONLY WAS THE SOUND GONE BUT EVERYTHING WAS STILL AS DEATH.

I LOOKED AT MY FRIEND DR. JACOB ROYCE IN STARK DISBELIEF. HIS MOUTH WAS FROZEN IN THE ACT OF SPEAKING, AS IF HE HAD BEEN CHISELED IN MARBLE BY SOME MASTER SCULPTOR. HIS HAND WAS POISED OVER THE CHESSMAN, UNMOVING AND IMMOVABLE, AS THOUGH CAST IN BRONZE. OUTSIDE THE WINDOW, LIKE IN THE OLD CHILD'S GAME, PEOPLE HAD TURNED TO STATUES: A CAR BACKING INTO A PARKING SPACE WAS STOPPED IN ITS TRACKS, SLANTED AGAINST THE TRAFFIC WHICH HAD BEEN HALTED NOT BY IT, BUT BY SOME FORCE BEYOND UNDERSTANDING: OUTSIDE MY WINDOW, BEYOND MY WELL-LOVED AVOCADO TREE, THE VERY RAINDROPS HUNG MOTIONLESS IN THE AIR LIKE A SPANGLED CURTAIN. AND IN THAT AWFUL, TERRIFYING, APOCALYPTIC MOMENT I REALIZED WITH STARTLING

AND FRIGHTENING SUDDENNESS, THAT
FOR EVERYONE ELSE IN THE WORLD,
SAVE ONLY ME AND THAT DAMNABLE
MACHINE...

TIME

        WAS

                STANDING

                        STILL!!!

* * * * * * * *

The next hour was a strange delirium. I found
myself more vital and alive than ever in my life. My
brain fairly raced with new ideas to achieve my
life-long dream: the construction of a perpetual motion timepiece. My legs were as supple and tireless as
an eighteen-year-old's as I climbed the stairs to the
bedroom floor. I gazed in awe at my wife, frozen in
the act of turning in her sleep, and, peeking into
Harriet's room, I saw her immobile on her back in
the middle of a gargantuan snore.

Like a child in some strange wonderland I came
downstairs, pausing at the bottom to listen. The only
other sound save my breathing and the strong, young
beat of my own heart, was the steady pulsation of the
eerie clock, running steadily. I had no doubts or
worries, somehow, that it would stop running, not

till the end of this hour, at least, so I wandered out the back door and into the streets.

Everywhere, there were frozen tableaux. Two cats on the backyard fence, one crouched menacingly, the other with its back arched high and its fur bristling: a man caught in the act of opening his bedroom window to ventilate the room; it had stopped raining and a man was arrested in the process of taking down his umbrella, while from the eaves the drops of water hung in the air, motionless; two drunks on their way home were in a preposterous pose, one in the act of falling, the other reaching in a desperate grab, forever too late; a bum stooping to pick up something was a mad caricature of an athlete poised to start a race; and the moon which had been coming out of the clouds seemed to be caught in some vast cosmic spiderweb. I wandered in a daze of ecstasy, filled with this enormous sense of power. I was the only thing that moved in the world. Except the clock. And suddenly, a quick stab of terror prodded at me. It must be nearing the end of the hour. What was to happen then? Or even more terrifying to contemplate—was this to be forever?

Returning to the store, nothing had changed. Poor Jake sat, like the Tin Woodman, stopped in the middle of the move that he had started nearly an hour before. The hands of all the clocks on the wall pointed to exactly twelve—except the hourglass one. In the stillness, my own heart seemed to be beating as loudly as its did. The hour hand stood directly at that mysterious 13, while the minute hand swept closer and closer to join it. With a sense of mounting excitement I waited for that junction. The suspense was unbearable. Unlike the other clocks, my strange, new acquisition had not struck *twelve* times, just one single chime. Now I felt I knew the reason for that numeral thirteen, and *why* the clock had struck only once. That was its magic gift to its owner. One priceless hour of precious time twice a day. With baited breath, I waited for the proof.

At last it came. That strange, haunting chime so like a slightly sorrowful, but mocking laugh.

One. how to describe the sound?

Two. Inhuman. Well, of course.

Three. Supernatural. Definitely.

Four. Hollow—echoing—as from the grave.

Five. Taunting, teasing, like the Lorelei.

Six. It was a laugh; I could recognize that more and more.

Seven. But an enemy's laugh, laughing at, not with.

Eight. Was I going crazy, or was it somehow menacing?

Nine. Why? When it had given me what was more precious than gold?

Ten. Did it want something in return?

Eleven. I was sweating, but I felt like ice. Now I knew the word: *Diabolical!*

222

Diabolical!

Twelve.—

And on that instant all the clocks came alive again, ticking, tocking and finishing their chimes.

And on the same instant my good friend Jake completed his move and his sentence:

"... erately set up the board in this madhouse tonight to get me off my game."

He pushed his chair back with a grunt.

"Ah, the hell with it. I concede."

"Don't you want some more time to think it over?"

The question was really to test him. Had he noticed anything unusual? His answer reassured me.

"It wouldn't matter if you gave me an hour to think it over. I'm too bushed to think." He yawned prodigiously. "Look at that! Not even one minute after twelve. We've only been playing fifteen minutes, and I feel as if it were seventy-five."

Again I eyed him carefully.

"Has it really only been fifteen minutes?" I asked.

"You're the clockmaker, Ethan," he laughed at me. "Look around at all your little markers."

"Yes—yes, you're right. So it's true."

I was scarcely aware of having said the last. It had been below my breath, but Jake was as sharp as a tack, and he picked it up.

"You feeling all right, Ethan?"

"Never better," I remonstrated quickly. "Why?"

"You looked a little strange for a minute. Matter of fact, I've been meaning to mention it. Like to have you drop around to the office some day soon."

"What for?"

He pushed back his chair, speaking with a careful casualness as he rose a little stiffly.

"You're not as young as you were, you know, and you push yourself pretty hard."

"Well, business has been pretty slow," I said, rising.

"I know, I know." He cocked his head, squinting at me, wisely. "And there's the strain of a wife who's always sick and that ring-tailed witch, Harriet." He moved towards the door and I followed. "Nothing to be alarmed about, Ethan. Just want to check you out. Want to make a date now?"

"I'll call you."

"Don't forget!"

As I reached to open the door, his eye fell on my giant avocado in the window, and he chuckled:

"Now there's something I wish all my patients were as healthy as."

I never can talk about that tree without pride.

"Twenty years since I started her in the window there."

"And like Topsy, 'it just growed,' mmm?"

"Don't you believe it! Took a lot of tender, loving care. Watering it just right, pinching it back, nursing it through funguses and other diseases, bringing it along slow but steady so's it'd grow up just right. Just like a child. I love that old tree."

"A man's got to have *something* to love, Ethan! I've got my patients, what have you got?"

"My clocks I guess. Though I won't say I wouldn't have liked a child." I pushed that thought away from me quickly, and looked fondly at my tree. "I guess she'll just have to do, Jake." I opened the door for him. "Night Jake."

"Night, Ethan. Hmm. Rain's stopped."

He hesitated a moment, looking up at the sky. A good man, I thought to myself, and now there was really no-one else I was close to. It was a fine moment in life to know that I had at least one friend. Then, the spell was broken, as he started to move and I found myself blurting out:

"Jake?"

"Yes, Ethan."

"You don't think there's anything serious wrong with Henny?"

"No, Ethan. Just one of her eternal spells. Don't you worry."

For a long time after my old friend drove away, I stood by the door, gazing out into the cool crisp night. I didn't notice the cold. I was too full of a bubbling excitement welling up inside me. A whole new world was mine! I was richer than any king! What an Emperor's ransom the clock had brought me! The dreams were building like castles in my head. What I would do with my borrowed time, the freedom it would bring me from—

"From just what," was never finished. Harriet's rasping voice, behind me, interrupted.

"Have you taken leave of your senses, Ethan Vigil? Close that door before you freeze us all to death and burn up every drop of oil in the tank."

"Yes Harriet," I said meekly, and obeyed her. But she wasn't finished yet.

"With oil costing what it does, and all these lights burning! You want to make the utility company rich while you waste every penny we've got?"

"No, Harriet."

"No thought for anyone but yourself! My poor invalid sister laying up there on her bed of pain, and this toothache, a cross that nobody should be asked to bear, and all you do is—"

Long before she had finished with her tirade, I had closed my ears to it. You learn to do that kind of thing when you live with someone like Harriet. Her voice went on like a buzzsaw, ripping and tearing, but it was faraway, a voice in a bad dream. That irritating, whining tone no longer grated on me, turning my stomach sour. Nor did the prospect of my usual night spent on the edge of the bed, afraid to move lest I wake up Henrietta to a new stream of complaint that tied my nerves in knots. For now I knew, no matter what, for two blessed hours every day from here on in, I was a free man! And the only thing I heard that night as my head hit the pillow, was the triumphant beat of the clock sounding in my inner ear. Or was it the sound of my own heart?

I was the happiest, luckiest man in the world, and I gloried in it.

* * * * * * * *

I should have known better than to fly in the face of Fate, or to think for a moment that anybody ever got something for nothing.

During the next week, Henny's complaints increased, if that was possible. And day by day she grew weaker. We had to call in Jake Royce, and after grumbling some, he came. I was in my shop this particular day that he examined Henrietta, and I heard his conversation with Harriet after he came downstairs.

"I don't mean to alarm you, Harriet, but I'm going to put your sister in the hospital."

"What's the matter with her, doctor?"

"That's what I want to put her in the hospital for. To find out."

"Hospitals are so expensive!"

"So are funerals. And you don't come home from those."

I could hear Harriet gasp.

"Then it's serious?"

"Now I shouldn't have said what I did." It was

227

the first time I ever heard Jake Royce sound contrite. "I don't know. I hope not. Why don't you go up and keep her company while I talk to Ethan?"

"You won't have any trouble convincing him! That man can find any way to waste money. I don't see why I can't nurse her myself!"

"Well, you can't this time, Harriet!" Jake's voice had a real bite to it, and the ring of authority. "You want to help, go sit with her a while and try to reassure her. If you can!"

"Yes doctor. If you say so."

She went off obediently enough up the stairs, and I reflected to myself what a pity it was *I* couldn't cut her down to size the way *Jake* did. By that time Jake had come in to tell me about the hospital, and I told him I'd overheard. I couldn't help repeating Harriet's concern:

"She's really that sick, Jake?"

"I'm not sure. This isn't just one of her spells. She ought to be under observation for a while."

"Whatever you say."

"I wish I knew *what* to say. I feel kinda guilty. Ever since that night last week when we were playing chess."

"What do you mean—'guilty'," I asked.

"Well, dammit to Hell, Ethan. For well over twenty years I've been medicating her imaginary ills, feeding her placebos and pink pills made of sugar. Now I wonder if mebbe I was somehow careless. For there's no doubt on the evidence that this debility, anemia, whatever you want to call it, started in around that night." He shook his head unhappily and sighed, throwing his shoulders back. "Well, no sense moping over spilt milk. I'll get along and make all the arrangements. I'll phone you when to expect the ambulance."

After he'd gone, I found my own guilt nagging at me. Ever since I'd discovered the secret of the clock, I'd thought of pretty near nothing else. I'd waited, eager as a child, for those two stolen hours every day. Not only for the relief from Harriet's nagging, poor Henrietta's whining, never-ending complaints, and the constant struggle just to make ends meet; but mainly for the lift, the joy, the burst of youth and vigor those special times brought me. For I'd gone one better than Ponce de León—for one twelfth of a day every day anyway. After all, he only went seeking the Foutain of Youth. *I'd found it!*

But once again I'd allowed the dream to lull me into a false sense of security. Because a wave of shocks was about to jolt me back to reality. The first was Henny's being taken to the hospital.

The second was the morning the clock stopped!

I was frantic. My golden hours of solitude gone! My extra gift of priceless time and the rebirth of youth? I couldn't let that go. There must be some way to bring them back, to start that damned intricate mechanism again. I tried everything I could think of.

Delicacy.

Using my finest precision instruments, probing, manoeuvering, trying to reach into those secret works. Magnifying glass, power magnification, flexible shafts, working blind, hoping to read something, find something, trip something to start that diaphragm hidden in the lower half of the hourglass, pumping again.

Failure. So I resorted to:

Power.

Drills, rasp bits, a router, electric chisel. Everything I could think of to break through the case and get at the motive power inside.

Failure. So next I went to:

Heat.

Blowtorch, acetylene torch, electric etcher, a welder's gun. I didn't have a laser beam, but I doubted if that would work. Once again:

Failure. And so to the court of last resort:

Brute strength.

Hammers, mauls, cold chisels, a diamond blade circular saw!

Failure. Nothing, nothing would pierce or cut or shatter the casing that hid the secret of the clock. Not even those glass windows, which were only an illusion. Whatever they were made of they were as impervious to any of my tools as the rest of it. I was frantic—in a kind of suicidal frenzy—and then, suddenly all the clocks started to strike the twelve strokes of midday. I found myself arrested, waiting with bated breath, hoping against hope—

But suddenly all was silence. It was just as I thought. The clock was dead, its life blood somehow drained—!

Blood! That's the whole answer! That's what started it in the first place. Maybe if—

The shrill sound of the telephone bell broke in. I didn't want to answer it, but somehow it had a voice of its own, demanding, threatening me. I picked up the receiver.

"Ethan, it's Jake."

"Oh. Look Jake. I don't want to talk now."

"Then you've heard?"

"Heard what?"

"About Henrietta."

A hand seemed to fasten itself about my throat, constricting my voice, making it hoarse.

"What about Henny?"

"I just got back to my office and there was a message waiting for me to call the hospital." His voice was suddenly very soft and gentle. "I'm sorry, Ethan, but she's gone. She passed away."

"I'll be right over to the hospital."

"I'll meet you there."

I hung up, numbly. It was a long time since there had been that much love between Henny and me. But

231

we also had a long life stretching backwards together. I was sick to my soul, and ashamed that in
my own selfish preoccupation, she had been so far out
of my mind. I pulled myself together and left.

When I got there, I sat by a nurses' desk, waiting
for Jake to complete arrangements and drive me
home. My mind was empty except for the constant
refrain. Henny was gone. With no goodbyes. I
came too late. Idly, I watched a young nurse come
down the hall with a tray of blood samples. She put
them on the desk and came to me.

"Mr. Vigil?"

"Yes."

"Dr. Royce asked me to tell you he'll only be a few
minutes longer."

"Thank you, nurse."

She walked away, while I sat in a stupor. I didn't
realize I was looking at *anything*, but suddenly, as
though a focus knob had been turned, as bright as
any picture in an advertisement for a product, I was
looking at that tray of blood samples.

Blood!

It was an explosion that left my mind crystal
clear. It was Henny's cutting her finger that started
the clock! Could that be the answer? I acted without
thinking. In a moment I was by that sample tray on
the desk, and had slipped one of the tubes into my
pocket.

I was back in my seat before Jake came striding down the hall to drive me home.

I couldn't wait for him to leave, and to be alone, after we got back there. The moment he was gone, I was in the shop, locking the door behind me. I rushed to the clock. My hand was shaking as I lifted the lid, exposing the brain (or whatever it was), while with the other, I slipped out the cork from the test tube. Then I poured in the blood, prepared to wait, but there was no need.

FOR IMMEDIATELY, WITH A THIRSTY, SUCKING SOUND, THE BLOOD WAS DRAWN INTO THE BODY OF IT, WHILE AT THE SAME TIME THERE WAS A WHIRRING AS THE HANDS WENT SPINNING AROUND TO THE PROPER TIME AND THEN:

The clock was alive again—Its heart was beating!

(But it would have been better, far better, had I left it for dead. As I would have, I believe, or like to tell myself I believe, if I had known then what I know now.)

* * * * * * *

The saddest part of all my confession is, that after my wife's death, I was even more blind to everything except those two periods of escape each day. More and more my sister-in-law Harriet took over the ordinary side of life, transforming my beloved clock shop into a nightmare of claptrappery to which I preferred to close my eyes. But I couldn't always close my ears as successfully.

"Ethan? Ethan!"

"What, Harriet?"

"Would you mind helping me with this window please?"

"What's the matter with the window?"

"If you'd just get away from that bench of yours for a moment and come here, I'll show you."

Oh, that rasping, teeth-tingling voice! Anything to still it. I rose and went to the display window, protesting weakly:

"Harriet, all right. But if you expect me to get my watch repairs done—"

"That piddling business!" She cut me off with her disdain. "That isn't enough to keep a roof over our heads, even with poor Henny gone to her reward." She paused a moment for the appropriate look of loss and sorrow. Then, charged ahead, refueled. "Now that *I'm* the active partner in the store, I've decided to branch out."

I couldn't hide my dismay and dislike.

"With all that gimcrack jewelry and cheap gew-gaws?"

"You're just way behind the times. This is novelty jewelry, it's what people buy, only, in order to sell it we have to display it."

234

"Cheap claptrap."

That produced a sniff. And when Harriet sniffs, it's the putdown complete.

"What about all those old rickety, broken-down clocks no sane person would buy any more?"

"These were made by craftsmen. They may be old-fashioned, but by Trophet, they stand for something! A man could take pride in dealing and servicing them."

"Stuff and nonsense. The world's just passing you by, Ethan Vigil. Now, first-off, I want you to get this cheap, old rubber plant out of the window—"

She stopped suddenly, maybe because she saw my face, or sensed the murder that welled up inside me. Damn! The woman was talking about the nearest thing to a child I—but by that time I found myself answering, and mighty hot under the collar.

"*Rubber plant!* Woman, that's an avocado tree I grew with my own hands from seed!"

"Well, whatever it is. It takes up the whole window. I want it out of here."

"Nosir! Not my tree. It needs every bit of sunshine it gets."

"But what use is it?"

"Tarnation, woman. Must everything have a function! It's beautiful, and it is balm to my soul. That's reason enough for its existence. And since it don't cost nothing, *you just leave it alone!*"

I guess I hadn't realized quite how vehement I'd

gotten, for to my surprise, Harriet backed down as meekly as if I'd been Dr. Jacob Royce at his most forbidding.

"All right, Ethan. But I have to have somewhere to display my costume jewelry. Let's move that ugly old hour glass piece of junk you bought from that drunken sot. Why does that have to be right there on your bench, just where every customer who comes in could look and see my jewelry? I ought to throw it out with the rubbish."

"Harriet!" I guess, once again, the amount of feeling in back of my words got through even her thick armor. "I'm warning you! You leave that clock where it is, and don't you ever *dare* lay a hand on it!"

I must have been quite menacing, for again she backed off, curling her lip as she said:

"My, aren't we touchy! All right. But just let me remind you of something, Ethan Vigil. With Henrietta gone, her share reverts to me, so I am two-thirds of this store. I can have it any way I want it!"

"Over my dead body! You can do what you want with all your cheap tinselly stuff, but keep your hands off my tree and this clock! Understand?"

Her shrug was eloquent, but I didn't care about reading its meaning. I only waited for her reply.

"Heaven's sakes, what a fuss. All *right*!"

At that moment all the clocks began to whirr into

striking the half hour. Harriet seemed almost relieved.

"Half past eleven already," she said. "Don't you have an appointment with Dr. Royce?"

"Dammall," I answered, "I forgot. Better get over there right away."

"Don't worry," Harriet carolled after me, all sweetness and light, "I'll take care of the store."

At Ethan's office, we went through the whole ritual, and finally he grumphed to me.

"Okay, Ethan, you can put your shirt back on."

"What's the verdict?" I asked as I struggled back into it.

"I couldn't be more pleased." This from Jake the iconoclast? And the funny thing was, he seemed sincere.

"You mean you like the shape I'm in?"

He chuckled, looking at me, and winked in old companionship.

"Look, you sour, cantankerous, lugubrious-looking old, long-jawed downeaster, you still don't look a day younger than all the years I know you carry! But by damn, your insides are running as sweet as any of your favorite clocks. What's your secret?"

"What do you mean?"

"I mean before Henrietta died, I was plumb worried about you. Your heart was acting up, I didn't like your blood pressure, and there was a lump in your belly I could palpate, big as a grapefruit."

237

"And now?"

"Now, I don't even need the X-rays I took. Know it before I see them. The lump is gone, your blood pressure's down, and your heart's as steady as a bell. Phew! Practically noon. Go on, get out of here! You don't need a doctor. Let me get to the sick people who do!"

AS I WENT INTO THE OUTER OFFICE, I GLANCED AT THE ELECTRIC CLOCK ON THE WALL. THE HANDS CLICKED TO NOON AS I DID SO, AND I WAS LOOKING AT A BY NOW FAMILIAR SCENE. THE NURSE WHO HAD RISEN TO ESCORT THE NEXT PATIENT IN, WAS SUDDENLY TRANSFIXED HALF-WAY UP FROM HER CHAIR. A CHILD ABOUT TO SCREAM REMAINED WITH FACE CONTORTED, THE SCREAM NOT YET UTTERED. A MAN LIGHTING A CIGARETTE POSED WITH A MATCH ON THE WAY TO HIS FACE, THE FLAME DRAWN BY A CARTOONIST. A THOUGHT CROSSED MY MIND. IT WAS A MONTH SINCE I HAD FED THE CLOCK ITS TRANSFUSION. I SHOULD PROTECT US BOTH. I WENT INTO JAKE'S SMALL LAB AND OPENED THE REFRIGERATOR. ONE SHELF WAS FILLED WITH BLOOD SAMPLES, NEATLY LABELED. I HELPED

238

MYSELF TO A FEW AT RANDOM, AND LEFT.

Back at the store, the only sound was the beat of my clock. Was it my fancy, or did it seem labored?

For the moment a blind fury diverted my attention as I looked at what Harriet had done since I left. Draped all over my avocado tree, were festoons of cheap bead and glass jewelry, and Harriet, a superior smirk on her face, was caught immobile in the act of adding more. But my anger choked back suddenly on itself, because at that moment, the clockbeat faltered and died.

For a moment my own heart skipped a beat—and then I remembered my lucky foresight. I rushed and got one of the vials of blood, hurried back to the bench. The lid on the clock gave its little protesting shriek as I opened it, and with shaking fingers, I emptied the vial of blood into the bowels of the thing.

And immediately, the vampire clock started to life!

So, the pattern of my life for the following months was set. The part of it in my waking moments, became only a necessary bridge between those hours of infinite relief and accomplishment my clock provided me with each noon and midnight. My designs for my perpetual motion clock were already completed. I had started to build the prototype. That was my real life, and I thanked the clock in my

239

heart for providing me with it, except that I found to my dismay that the clock seemed to demand more and more frequent transfusions to keep running. But these were easy to secure from Jake's office in those hours when time stood still for everyone save me.

And then, once again events caught up with me, and this time the revelation was total disaster!

It was an evening after dinner, working alone in my shop. For once, clocks and *the* clock were of less concern to me than my avocado tree. For the last week now it had been failing, the leaves turning brown and limp, and no remedy I tried seemed able to renew its accustomed vigor. I was dusting it carefully with a new powder, when I saw Jake's car draw up at the curb, and a moment later he was tapping at the window. I moved to the door to let him in.

"Jake! What're you doing here this time of night?"

"Oh, the evening's young," he said as he entered and I closed the door behind him. I thought he looked tired and worried, and he seemed preoccupied, although his next words appeared to disprove that. "Thought a chess game might get some things off my mind. Speaking of that, what you got on yours? What were you frowning at when I tapped on the window?"

"My plant there."

"The avocado? Yep. Does look a mite peaked."

"Can't understand it. All of a sudden it started to wilt like that. You any good at diagnosing vegetable life, Jake?"

He shook his head and sighed heavily.

"Nope. And to tell you the truth I'm not much good at my *own* job. Wish I knew the secret of your spurt of youth. Getting old I guess."

"We might just be able to mend that with a little medicine *I* have in the back. Let's go in by the fire and inject it."

For just a second there was a twinkle in my old friend's eye at the prospect, and as he preceded me into the back parlor, he seemed momentarily less dejected. I left him to poke up the fire, while I went to brew our toddy.

When I came back he was sitting staring into the fire, but he perked up a bit as I handed him his mug. We lifted them in a silent toast as I sat down, and he drank deep. After letting the brew rest on his tongue a moment, he swallowed it with a long, satisfied exhalation of breath.

"Ah, that's good, Ethan! Nothing like a hot Tom and Jerry on a winter's night in Boston, when old blood is running stiff and cold."

And once again, with those words, he slipped back into melancholy again.

"You're not yourself, Jake," I said. "What's wrong?"

241

"I don't exactly know. In a way it goes back to Henrietta's death. Or seems to."

What does?"

He didn't answer for a moment, gathering his thoughts, as it were. Before he began, as if he needed the support, he took a deep swig of his drink. Then, as if with difficulty, he brought his eyes up to mine.

"Ethan," he said, "I never said much at the time about the way Henrietta died."

"Congestive heart failure is what you told me."

"Oh, that's true enough, as far as it goes. That's the condition that terminated her life." He leaned forward now, almost as though asking me the question directly, instead of rhetorically. "But what caused it—what created that condition?"

"Are you asking me?"

He shook his head and sank back deep in his chair, cradling the mug in his hands as if to draw strength from its warmth. His tone was bleak and self-accusatory.

"No. I'm asking myself. And I still have no answer. Oh, tests were run, and the pathologic evidence was clear enough."

"You want to make that so I can understand it?" I replied dryly.

"I can explain the word. Tests showed us, that in spite of massive transfusions, we couldn't stop your wife's blood from simply—" he searched a moment for a word, and settled on "simply disintegrating. A

242

massive anemia, pernicious and devastating! Quite literally, turning her blood to water!"

I couldn't tell him that he was practically doing the same thing to mine. I stammered out:

"But what was the cause?

"That's the whole question. I've never seen a case like it before. I should change that to say I *had* never seen a case. One would have been bad enough but—" he stopped to take a deep breath, then abandoning that line of thought for the moment, pulled himself together into the brisk, pragmatic man he usually was. "I came here tonight, Ethan, because I want you and Harriet at my office tomorrow morning for blood tests. I have every reason now to think that whatever Harriet had, it could be at least contagious. I pray not infectious. The damn thing seems epidemic enough as it is."

"Epidemic?"

He nodded his head abruptly, squaring his jaw. I could almost hear his teeth grind.

"In the last three months I've lost three of my patients to the same sort of—what shall I say—*malady*. What concerns me is a strange and inexplicable circumstance. Perhaps, the better word is coincidence."

I was discovering that my breathing had grown shallow. I seemed to be reaching for oxygen, and more than that, although I didn't fully understand yet, reassurance.

"What coincidence?" I asked.

"Each of these patients had been to my office for routine physicals. I might have spotted the onset of this thing, whatever it is, except for a curious fact. All of them had left blood samples to be worked up in the lab."

Even my throat was closing up on me. I took a quick drink, clearing my throat and queried:

"The blood samples didn't warn you?"

"They couldn't very well, since there were none to examine. Unaccountably, they had all disappeared from my office. Oh, and one other strange coincidence. The night Henrietta died was the first night a blood sample disappeared. Not from my office, but from the hospital."

"And that patient died later also?"

"That's right." He suddenly pulled himself out of a slump, draining the rest of his drink and putting the mug aside. "About four weeks later." He stood up abruptly. "I don't know why I'm bothering you about this. It's none of your business."

I stood up with more difficulty than he, wondering if I could talk. My throat felt as if some massive vegetable growth was smothering not only my vocal cords, but my breathing.

"But it is," I managed to get out, without being too obviously in difficulty. "I mean it's my problem as much as yours."

244

Jake frowned in puzzlement for a moment. Then: "Oh you mean as far as Henrietta is concerned?"

"No!" I blurted out, "I mean more than that. I mean—" I stopped, facing the enormity of trying to explain, and lost, not only how to do it, but where even to begin. Jake answered me in quick concern.

"Ethan! What is it? I didn't mean to upset you!"

"I'm not upset. That is, I just want you to understand!"

"Understand what?"

I wasn't up to it!

I didn't have the courage. Or perhaps, if I can say anything in my own defense, I didn't know fully how to explain yet what I only suspected. So, my reply was a lame one.

"That—that I'm sorry, Jake." Then, with an amount of feeling that really choked me, "Oh, *I am sorry!*"

Jake accepted my emotion as concern for him. I'm ashamed to say I let him make that mistake. He put his arm around me for a moment and said:

"You're a good friend, Ethan. I guess we'll skip the chess tonight. I ought to get along. But don't forget—I want you and Harriet in my office in the morning!"

For a split second he gave me an affectionate hug, and then was on his way out. I couldn't let him go like that. I *had* to say something.

"Jake!"

"Yes?"

He stopped and turned while I fumbled to know what it was I wanted to say. What came out was:

"I never asked before. Do you remember exactly what time Henny died?"

"Since I signed the death certificate, yes. About twenty-five minutes to twelve, I think."

But I didn't *have to think*, after I let him go. Because at that particular moment I didn't have the courage to do anything else. *Twenty-five minutes to twelve!* Precisely to the moment that was the first time that evil clock stopped.

So now I knew the truth!

It was a vampire clock!

A MONSTER, INSATIABLE, THAT HAVING ONCE TASTED BLOOD, CONTINUED TO SUCK ITS VICTIM TILL IT HAD DRAINED ALL LIFE AWAY. AND I WAS NO BETTER, NO LESS EVIL. I HAD BEEN FEEDING THIS MECHANICAL LEECH AT THE COST OF OTHER HUMAN LIVES!

So, that was the past. Now I had to turn and face the future. The shop was dark as I walked to the clock. My ears were so attuned to it by now, that as I saw Jake out, I had realized that it had begun to labor, calling for a fresh transfusion.

And there, in the dark, I stood over it, half-mad for the moment as I hissed out loud:

"Die! Damn you forever, you devil, die!"

246

And as I said it, the heart-beat of the clock started slowly to fade, until, almost as if I had willed it, it was finally still. At its silence, I felt a surge of relief and, yes, of triumph!

* * * * * * * *

But my triumph was short-lived. I still had my own expiation to make. Not only for my wife, but for all those others. Still in the dark, I abandoned myself for a few moments to regrets. My hands traced sadly in the gloom the shape of my perpetual-motion machine, nearly finished but doomed never to be. I fought the sentiment, but in this moment of revelation, I had to view myself clearly: a man without love, without wife, or even children: a man who would have liked to leave one small footprint on the sands of eternity, one small gage to immortality. All I would leave now, was a dying avocado tree I had nourished and nursed for twenty-five years. It was too much for me, at this moment, and I sank down at my desk, my head buried in my hands, alone in the darkness of the room, and the darkness of despair.

I was only half-consciously aware that a door opened somewhere, and a shaft of light fell into the shop, not illuminating me, and doused as quickly as a candle by the door closing again. I heard the sluff-sluff-sluff of a woman's slippers across the floor, a lid removed from a can, the hiss of an aerosol spray. I reached forward quickly and clicked on the nearest light.

Harriet stood revealed by my avocado tree. In her hand was a spray can which she had been directing into the pot and the root of my avocado tree! For a moment I didn't know whether the blood-red cloud that was swimming before my eyes was from the sudden light, or what I felt in my heart: murder, sheer simple murderous rage!

"What are you doing to that plant?"

Her mouth had fallen open in a slack-lipped expression that would have been ludicrous under other circumstances. She tried to pull herself together.

"Why I—just some food for the tree that I—"

I tore the can from her hand.

"Let me see that!" As I read the lable, the red fog was there again, and I could feel bile rising in my throat. "It's a weed-killer! It's you! It's been you! You've been *poisoning* my tree! Why, you consummate bitch!"

"Don't you touch me, you—"

"You'll be lucky if I don't tear you limb from limb. *Get away from my tree!*"

In a blind rage now, I grabbed her by the arm and almost literally hurled her across me, and away from the tree. Spinning, she lost a bedroom slipper, half tripping over it and crashing into my work bench. As she did so, she reached instinctively for anything to support her, and in so doing grabbed the clock.

They fell to the floor together, heavily. Somehow, the hinged top had opened, and Harriet's hand had slipped inside it. Now she scrambled to her feet in triumph, throwing the clock on to the bench and away from her. She was screaming hysterically:

"All right, so I've poisoned your precious avocado tree! Only way to get rid of it! Just as I've now smashed up your ugly old clock! You wouldn't ever have taken that tree out of the window as I asked. So I've been poisoning it for weeks. And now, it's as good as dead right now!"

With that she picked up her slipper, and sucking on a finger, marched self-righteously out of the room, as I watched in creeping horror.

"And so are you, Harriet," I murmured to myself, "as good as dead. And what can I do about it?"

For lying on the floor, the monster clock, the insatiable vampire, the deadliest killer of them all, had started to beat once again! It had stolen blood from Harriet's finger, just as it had from Henrietta's, sealing Harriet's doom, as inevitably.

What is there left to say?

I will have to watch another human being die, slowly, inexorably, unable to arrest the inevitable. And even though it is someone I have every reason to despise, my guilt is in no way lessened.

The only pleasure I can derive, the only justification, is that as Harriet sinks, so does that remorseless, evil, damnable machine.

AND ONCE ITS HEART IS STILLED, I SHALL TAKE WHAT STEPS I CAN TO MAKE SURE IT IS STILLED FOREVER. THE ONE ELEMENT I HAVE YET TO TRY AGAINST IT, IS THE TRUE ENEMY OF THE DEVIL.

WATER!

I SHALL TAKE IT, CHAINED TO MY BODY, WHEN I GO TO MY OWN GRAVE IN THE RIVER. I INTEND TO MAKE IT *OUR* GRAVE, TO SHARE FOR ALL ETERNITY.

So, as I finish this confession, and sign it, and prepare it to be mailed to my dear friend Dr. Jacob Royce, I am listening to that unclean abomination, labor, struggle, to avoid another death. But this time I shall make certain it starves and suffocates and chokes on the lack of what it needs to feed on.

There. It has stopped. It is dead. It only remains for me to bury it with me.

STILL, BE WARNED! IF YOU EVER SHOULD COME ACROSS A CLOCK IN A CURIO SHOP, SHAPED LIKE AN HOURGLASS, WITH A DIAL THAT BEARS THE NUMERAL 13 INSTEAD OF 12, SHUN IT, I BEG YOU, LIKE THE PLAGUE!

Signed: Ethan Vigil.

All Time Bestsellers From Popular Library

☐ THE HALLELUJAH TRAIL, Bill Gulick   #00336 – $1.25

☐ THE HUNTING VARIETY,
Richard Flanagan   #00315 – $1.25

☐ JUMP CUT, R. R. Irvine   #00574 – 95c

☐ THE KAPPILLAN OF MALTA,
N. Monsarrat   #08354 – $1.95

☐ THE LAST CATHOLIC IN AMERICA,
J. R. Powers   #00199 – $1.25

☐ THE LATE GREAT CREATURE,
B. Brower   #00187 – $1.25

☐ THE LILIES OF THE FIELD, W. E. Barrett   #00677 – 95c

☐ LOOKING FOR FRED SCHMIDT,
Seymour Epstein   #08423 – $1.75

☐ THE PURSUIT OF LOVE/ LOVE IN A
COLD CLIMATE, Nancy Mitford   #08405 – $1.95

☐ MAN FRIDAY, Adrian Mitchell   #08420 – $1.25

☐ REGIMENT OF WOMEN, Th. Berger   #08330 – $1.75

☐ REMEMBER ME TO MARCIE,
Martin Yoseloff   #00327 – $1.25

☐ SHE WAITS, E. Fenton   #00283 – $1.25

☐ THE SPY, J. F. Cooper   #00302 – 95c

☐ SURFACING, M. Atwood   #03034 – $1.50

☐ TELL ME THAT YOU LOVE ME, JUNIE MOON,
M. Kellogg   #08223 – 95c

☐ THIRTY FOUR EAST, A. Coppel   #08357 – $1.95

☐ THREE PARTS EARTH, E. Frederikson   #00219 – $1.25

☐ THE TOOTH MERCHANT,
C. L. Sulzberger   #03053 – $1.50

☐ TO KILL A MOCKINGBIRD, Harper Lee   #08376 – $1.50

☐ THE WHOLE WORLD IS WATCHING,
A. Morgan   #03038 – $1.50

☐ THE WILBY CONSPIRACY, P. Driscoll   #08379 – $1.75

☐ WITCH TIDE, Charles Mercer   #03097 – $1.50

☐ A PATCH OF BLUE, E. Kata   #00303 – $1.25

☐ A PORTION FOR FOXES,
J. McIlvaine Mc Clary   #03001 – $1.50

☐ ADVANCING PAUL NEWMAN,
Eleanor Bergstein   #08438 – $1.75

☐ ALL VISITORS MUST BE ANNOUNCED,
H. Van Slyke   #00185 – $1.25

☐ ATLANTA, R. Dennis   #03064 – $1.50

☐ THE BLESSING & DON'T TELL ALFRED,
Nancy Mitford   #08440 – $1.95

☐ BY GRAND CENTRAL STATION I SAT
DOWN AND WEPT, E. Smart   #03083 – $1.50

☐ THE CASTLE ON THE RIVER,
C. Mercer   #00258 – $1.25

☐ CATS AND OTHER PEOPLE, T. Hohoff   #00589 – 95c

☐ THE DEFECTION OF A. J. LEWINTER,
R. Littel   #03010 – $1.50

Buy them at your local bookstore or use this handy coupon for ordering:

BOB-37

Popular Library, P.O. Box 5755, Terre Haute, Indiana 47805

Please send me the books I have checked above. I am enclosing $_____
(please add 35c to cover postage and handling). Send check or money order
—no cash or C.O.D.'s please. Orders of 5 books or more postage free.

Mr/Mrs/Miss_____

Address_____

City_____ State/Zip_____

Please allow three weeks for delivery. This offer expires 5/77.

SUPERNATURAL
.OCCULT

☐	KATIE KING: A Voice From Beyond, Gilbert Roller	– $1.50
☐	POSSESSION, C. Dane	– 75c
☐	PSYCHIC TRAVEL, C. Dane	– 95c
☐	SOME TRUST IN CHARIOTS, Ed. by B. Thiering and E. Castle	– 95c
☐	STRANGE ENCOUNTERS WITH GHOSTS, B. Steiger	– 75c
☐	STRANGE ESP, W. Smith	– 95c
☐	STRANGELY ENOUGH! C. B. Colby	– 95c
☐	SUPERNATURAL WARNINGS, R. Tralins	– 95c

Buy them at your local bookstore or use this handy coupon for ordering:

BOB-42

Popular Library, P.O. Box 5755, Terre Haute, Indiana 47805

Please send me the books I have checked above. I am enclosing $_____
(please add 50c to cover postage and handling). Send check or money order
—no cash or C.O.D.'s please. Orders of 5 books or more postage free.

Mr/Mrs/Miss_____

Address_____

City_____ State/Zip_____

Please allow three weeks for delivery. This offer expires 12/77.